MORE PRAISE FOR THE FOCUSED BUSINESS

"Dave Crenshaw is spot on with his assessment that chaos is a business killer. If we weren't able to focus and build the correct systems to avoid chaos, OtterBox wouldn't be the industry leader in mobile device protection."
— **CURT RICHARDSON**, founder and chairman, OtterBox

"The path of the entrepreneur is littered with every imaginable personal and professional struggle. Thank you, Dave, for showing how to overcome that chaos as entrepreneurs journey toward success."
— **ANISA TELWAR KAICKER**, founder and president, Anisa International

"Crenshaw outlines a winning game plan for entrepreneurs in *The Focused Business*. Highly entertaining and enlightening!"
— **MARK EATON**, NBA All-Star, speaker and founder, 7ft4.com

PRAISE FOR DAVE'S PREVIOUS BOOKS

"Dave Crenshaw demonstrates how multitasking is, in fact, a lie that actually wastes time, energy, and money . . . 'Switchtasking,' as Dave calls it, not only uses up more of our resources, but it also diminishes our overall productivity."
— **CHUCK NORRIS**, actor and martial artist

"We live in an ADHD world. And I'm glad we do. But as Dave understands, the secret is to do one important thing at a time, with focus. If you can take the time to focus on his message, you'll be glad you did."
— **SETH GODIN**, author of *Tribes*

"At Zappos.com, our core values include pursuing growth and learning, doing more with less, and building a positive team and family spirit. Dave's message can resonate with anyone looking to live those values and make themselves invaluable."
— **TONY HSIEH**, CEO, Zappos.com

"*Invaluable* is the next logical step in career development. This story will show you step-by-step how to increase your value in the market and increase workplace harmony."
— **DANIEL H. PINK**, author of *A Whole New Mind* and *Drive*

"*Invaluable* bridges the gap between employee-manager relationships and productivity. Companies that implement this message not only stand to improve their bottom line but also make their work environments happier for everyone."
— **KEITH FERRAZZI**, author of *Who's Got Your Back* and *Never Eat Alone*

"If every busy professional could internalize Crenshaw's message in this book, we'd all get much more done in less time."
— **GINA TRAPANI**, lead editor at Lifehacker, author of *Upgrade Your Life*

"Every great CEO and rainmaker needs this book!"
— **JEFFREY J. FOX**, author of *How to Become a Rainmaker*

"A fresh take on the problem of timewasters in our corporate and personal lives, *The Myth of Multitasking* will change your paradigm about what is productive and what is not. I loved the concept of 'switchtasking' versus multitasking. A must-read for all."
— **HYRUM SMITH**, co-founder, Franklin Covey; CEO, Galileo

THE
FOCUSED
BUSINESS

How Entrepreneurs Can
Triumph Over Chaos

Dave Crenshaw

Publisher's Cataloging-In-Publication Data

Crenshaw, Dave, 1975-

    The focused business : how entrepreneurs can triumph over chaos / Dave Crenshaw.

    p. : ill. ; cm.

    ISBN: 978-0-9891936-0-3 (pbk.)
    ISBN-13: 978-0-9891936-1-0 (e-book)

    1. Small business--Management. 2. Entrepreneurship. 3. Success in business. I. Title.

HD62.7 .C74 2013
658.02/2   2013937187

"Invaluable," "Systems, Accountability, Motivation," and all Agents of Chaos character names are trademarks of Dave Crenshaw and Invaluable Inc.

Printed in the United States of America.

Published by Invaluable Press
Lehi, Utah, USA

Cover design by John Arce and Utku Lomlu
Interior formatting by John Arce
Agents of Chaos character design by Donny Gandakusuma and John Arce

CONTENTS

For my children

You have my love and support,
whatever you choose to focus on.

EVERY HERO HAS A BEGINNING

Consider for a moment the beginning of your entrepreneurial story.[1]

Where were you? What sparked that moment of borderline-insanity that whispered in your ear, "Go it alone!"

I'm a fan of comic and movie superheroes, so in this book, I'll be using that metaphor—a lot. Why?

You may be surprised how much entrepreneur and superhero stories have in common. As an entrepreneur, you are also a kind of hero. You have the capacity to not only shape your own life and destiny, but those of your family, employees, community, and, quite possibly, the world. You share more in common with these fabled heroes than you yet realize.

---

1. Don't believe you're an entrepreneur? That's okay. Whether you call yourself a business owner, freelancer, or just self-employed, trust me, I'm still talking about you. It will save us a lot of space, time, and maybe a tree or two.

One thing I've learned is that *every* hero has an origin story. I've found that every superhero—and entrepreneur—has his or her roots in four major themes: destiny, decision, adversity, or accident. I'll explain.

Some people arrive at entrepreneurship by way of **DESTINY** or fate. Like Superman, these people were born into it. They have business in their DNA. It's their good genes. Could you imagine Mark Cuban doing anything other than starting companies? You have entrepreneurship in your blood if you can't imagine doing anything else with your life.

Many entrepreneurs weren't born into it, but they start companies anyway. They make a conscious **DECISION** to make a difference, like Batman. They are good at spotting opportunities and learning the skills required in order to create markets. Debbie Fields has always been able to bake a great cookie, but she didn't know much about business until she turned her talent into a company.

Some of the greatest businesses are born in moments of **ADVERSITY**. You have a lot in common with the comic-hero Iron Man if the economy backed you into a corner, put a gun to your head, and practically forced you to start a business. You're also in very good company. Macy's, Disney, Revlon, and Converse are just a handful of great businesses born from the Great Depression. J.K. Rowling's adversity spurred her forward until Harry Potter was published and became a success.

Did you stumble on a great idea? Are you an entrepreneur by **ACCIDENT**? Maybe you were doing something else, or you were at work, when an idea struck that was so irresistible you felt as though you were compelled by an outside source to pursue it by starting a company. Spider-Man was bitten by a radioactive spider. Harry Coover recognized the unique adhesive properties of Super Glue while working on polymers for jet canopies. George de Mestral was inspired to create Velcro by annoying burrs that stuck to his clothes when he went hunting.

Whatever led you to where you are now, odds are that running your own business has now consumed your life. You know what only those in business for themselves can know: that joy, enthusiasm, freedom, exhaustion, misery, and pain can all be experienced, often, within a single day.

WHERE MY STORY BEGAN

Now that you have your entrepreneurial origin story in the front of your mind, allow me to share mine with you. My origin story is one of both adversity and decision.

All my life, I've been watching people start businesses. Some have succeeded; most have failed.

Many of the people who failed were playing the game of entrepreneurship without knowing the rules. I spent my childhood watching the people close to me waste tremendous amounts of time and money making mistakes with their businesses.

Watching my family and friends struggle with entrepreneurship formed my career in a big way. I learned from watching them that I never wanted to make the same mistakes they did. I told myself that I would learn from their mistakes. Learning from my family members' mistakes would mean that their struggles were not in vain after all.

What's funny is I never thought I would be an entrepreneur. I didn't want anything to do with business. In fact, when I was a kid, I wanted to be a movie director. Steven Spielberg was my Hollywood hero. I imagined myself standing on stage to accept my Oscar, just like him.

But fate had a different plan for me. It's a story in three acts.

Act one began the moment I jumped out of the womb. To sum up a very long story, I was a walking chaotic catastrophe. I was born with the combined blessing/curse of attention deficit hyperactivity disorder. In fact, to quote the psychologist who ran me through two tests, I am "freaking off the charts ADHD. If there were a fifth standard deviation [I'd] be in it." In other words, I was given a challenge from the very beginning that ravaged my focus and pulled me from interest to interest, from career to career. My battle for focus has always been very personal. And I am intimately and painfully acquainted with the many forms a lack of focus can take.

Act two of this story came as a result of a two-year mission with members of my faith. I spent many months in the inner city of Indianapolis, Indiana, helping people who were struggling with their day-to-day lives. These weren't people who were making mistakes in business but people who had made mistakes in life, like depending on other people—mostly the government—to help them. We served a lot of people who, no matter how much help they received, couldn't wean themselves off the hand-outs. And that was heartbreaking. I saw what happened when people relied on other people to help them.

Also, I was mentored and led during that time by a successful serial entrepreneur, Bart Payne. I saw in him a kind of "brilliant madness" that I somehow identified with yet didn't understand. So gradually, I had begun forming a strong opinion that entrepreneurship, done well, was a hand up out of poverty, not a handout.

Then began the third act of my story. The catalyst was a family member—my brother-in-law, actually. Ever heard of BlenderBottle? Maybe you have one. The business started with an idea as simple as putting a whisk in a bottle, and it became a multimillion dollar company, Sundesa. That's my brother-in-law and sister's company.

Long before BlenderBottle was born, I was a struggling freshman in college. Like many young students, especially the ADHD ones, I was struggling to choose a major. I was at my sister's house one afternoon, rambling about my many options, and my brother-in-law Steve chimed in: "You know, Dave, you can't go wrong with a business degree. It's like Chrysler and apple pie. It doesn't matter what you want to do with your life, a business degree will help you pull it off."

And so, safely, carefully, casually, I began my journey into the world of business and, ultimately, the throes of entrepreneurship.

Is the System Really the Solution?

At some point, early in my business education, I was exposed to the concept of business systems. This is the idea that most small businesses lack systems, processes, and procedures. Without these systems, the results are wildly inconsistent.

Something about this just clicked in my mind. Suddenly I saw a reason for all the entrepreneurial failure around me. Not only that, I saw a solution.

At the age of twenty-two, I took out a loan against my car, left college, and enrolled in a certification program originally designed to teach accountants how to transform small businesses. No, I was not an accountant. I was just crazy enough to think I could change the world, one entrepreneur at a time. I still think that.

Over time, though, I found this "system is the solution" philosophy had big chinks in its armor. Yes, all small businesses need systems—often desperately. However, focus too much on systems and you will miss out on the other two-thirds of the equation, specifically accountability and motivation. But more on that later.

Around the year 2000 I went rogue—independent. I began developing my own business coaching philosophy and methodology. By the time I finally completed a bachelor's in entrepreneurship, I had already coached dozens of small businesses one-on-one.

My continuing experience with entrepreneurs led me to tackle their consistent lack of time in my first book, *The Myth of Multitasking*, which has since been published in six languages. This opened the door for me to serve more and more businesses, both in private and public settings. It also led me to my second book, *Invaluable*, which was designed to help employees think more entrepreneurially.

As I've had the privilege now of serving thousands of entrepreneurs and their employees, my philosophy has become more and more targeted. I now see one primary cause of small business failure: a lack of focus.

So, this book is my PhD dissertation for the Entrepreneur's School of Hard Knocks. It is the culmination of my exploration, personal battles, and service to entrepreneurs like you up to this point. No fancy review board and defense in front of a panel of experts. This is just you and me having a conversation.

If you choose, it can also become your guidebook to help you build a focused, profitable, successful, and fulfilling small business.

How to Use and Abuse This Book

If you own more than one business, read this book while thinking only about your most valuable business. Think only about the one business that gives you the most profit, joy, and satisfaction.

Then later, if you're a crazed serial-entrepreneur-with-your-hands-in-multiple-businesses-bent-on-world-domination, return to this book again. You'll get better results if you can focus your reading from the beginning.

Also, I also want you to put your notebook away at first. If you must take notes, do it in the margins of the book, right between the covers. Don't worry. It's just a book. Fire is the only thing that will hurt it. (Or water, if you're reading this digitally!) Your ink is harmless.

This book isn't about ideas so much as it's about ideas that produce action. As you notate things, actions will come to mind. At the end of every chapter, I'll give you the opportunity to write down what you believe is the single most important action to take. Share these actions with your coach or mentor. Talk with other entrepreneurs about this book and the actions you're taking. Your public declarations will help create private accountability.

But, most important, *act* on your ideas as soon as possible. The sooner you act, the more success you'll experience. This book will only be as valuable as the action you take upon it.

Now, let's begin the next act of *your* story . . .

CHAPTER I

What Is Chaos?

Let's get right to the universal paradox of running a business. I call it the Law of Chaos.

You want to be successful in entrepreneurship, right? Of course you do!

But the universal paradox, the Law of Chaos, is this:

Business success breeds business chaos.

The more sales roll in, the more difficult it becomes to keep customers happy. The more employees you hire, the more you have to deal with management and daily drama. The more products or services you produce, the higher the likelihood of mistakes. And on and on.

Success then becomes the catalyst of chaos. Nearly every aspect of your business will show symptoms of chaos as it grows. Business success breeds business chaos.

As you grow, the resources you started with become inadequate. It's a matter of when, not if. What you started with six months ago no longer meets the needs of your growing customer base. As you get more customers, you need more people, more desks, more computers, more space, more time, and more *everything*. Having to do without these things causes chaos. Chaos manifests itself in your cash flow, staff, storefront, Internet presence, marketing, task list, personal life, and organization chart.

Chaos is pervasive in business. It's everywhere all at once. It is the first word, and it could get the last word if you're not careful. Chaos is the one constant presence in your life as an entrepreneur. The reason for this is that it affects all aspects of your business—every last one of them.

Not enough money? **CHAOS.**

Wrong employees? **CHAOS.**

Not enough employees? **CHAOS.**

Employees have no idea what to do? **CHAOS!**

The list of examples is endless. Chaos is the easiest trap in the world to fall into. Spending too much time prioritizing your million-mile list of things to do causes chaos. Answering hundreds of e-mails a day causes chaos.

In other, more stark, words:

YOUR DESIRE FOR SUCCESS AS AN ENTREPRENEUR IS ULTIMATELY SELF-TORTURE.

The irony of it all is that you told yourself life would be better as a business owner. You wouldn't have to answer to corporate anymore. Your days of pandering and posturing for customers and coworkers would finally be over! Right? All your problems would magically disappear once you started your own business, once you became an entrepreneur, once you controlled EVERYTHING.

And you did just that. In the beginning, it was a success. The business started making money and took off from there. You thought, *This is it! I'm free!*

But you didn't escape chaos, did you? You just created a different breed of the same beast.

Life hasn't truly changed. You're still pandering and posturing. You keep telling yourself it will get better as long as you keep working on your business. But your life is still a hot mess of melted, chaos-flavored ice cream all over your brand new sneakers.

The Law of Chaos is relentless. The more successful you are, the more chaos rules your life and your business. The more success you experience, the higher the odds of your failure. Don't believe me?

Imagine if 0.01 percent of planes that took off from airports around the world crashed, a paltry one in 10,000. This means that roughly ninety-three plane crashes would occur *every day*. You wouldn't even think about buying a ticket for that ride!

Yet entrepreneurs engage in even riskier behavior ... statistically speaking. Imagine if 50 percent of all small businesses failed. You don't have to imagine because that is, in fact, the failure rate for new businesses. According to data compiled by the U.S. Small Business Administration (SBA), 50 percent of all new businesses will fail within five years of launching. About 75 percent go up in flames by year fifteen.

Bankruptcy numbers continue to skyrocket for entrepreneurs. Recently a new and disturbing trend has also surfaced: according to the most recent reports from the SBA, more businesses are now *closing* each year than are opening. Every hour approximately sixty-eight businesses close their doors. Ouch.

I've found that the truth finally starts sinking in for entrepreneurs around year three of ownership, when the initial honeymoon glow has long since disappeared. There comes that moment, somewhere between year three and year six, when the Law of Chaos smacks you over the head. It's the three-year entrepreneurial itch. It's the point when you realize, *Things aren't getting better. They're getting worse.*

With no end in sight.

Who is to blame for all of this small business nastiness?

INTRODUCING CHAOS INC.

Ever driven around town and noticed all the businesses out there, most of which you have no idea what they do? CHAOS Inc. is just like that, except they're up to absolutely no good.

Their founder runs CHAOS Inc. out of an abandoned missile silo in the Midwest, supported by a team of IT pros who keep his supercomputers humming along. Some say he's ex-KGB. Others say he had a falling out with a US-based alphabet organization. The truth is, nobody knows where he came from. He's a ghost. He's a mystery.

I know one thing for sure about the head of CHAOS Inc. He knows what I know: most of the world's economic growth, success, and happiness starts with entrepreneurs. He knows that job security and financial stability for thousands of other individual starts with you, the person crazy enough to risk starting a business. Like any evil organization, CHAOS Inc. wants to stop you from achieving success with your business. CHAOS Inc. works around the clock, without sleep, to make sure your business fails.

CHAOS Inc. is the physical manifestation of chaos, the cause of most business failures.

DEFINING CHAOS

We need to define chaos before introducing key members of the staff at CHAOS Inc.

Chaos: The haphazard allocation of resources toward that which is of variable value.

Let's think about what that means for a second. You're working, you're allocating resources. You're working very hard, doing a lot of things all at the same time. When you're in a state of chaos, your work happens all over the place. A little here, a little there. In the middle of answering an e-mail, the phone rings. The phone rings again in the middle of the call. Maybe it's your delivery driver. His truck broke down. It's your job to fix it. You blow the rest of your day replacing tires and putting out fires on the road.

When you're operating in a state of chaos, some of the things you're working on are valuable. Other things you're working on, the fires you have to put out, are worth jack squat in terms of using your resources wisely.

At some point, it hits you. You start questioning yourself, asking yourself things like this:

"Oh. My. Gosh. Why on earth did I spend hours and weeks and months trying to build a new location? I didn't even need a second location. What the heck did I do to myself?"

When you spend a lot of time and effort developing some new scheme, only to ask, "Why did I do that?" when all is said and done, that's the haphazard allocation of resources at work. Everything to do with that unnecessary effort causes chaos. When you work furiously through your day, only to finish with asking yourself, "What did I do with the day?"—that's the haphazard allocation of resources, causing chaos in your business again.

The Motto

Have you got a company motto or slogan? CHAOS Inc. does. Their slogan, proudly displayed in black and gold letters at the doorway of their hidden bunker office is

C OMPANY
H AVOC
A ND
O WNER
S TRESS

Employees at CHAOS Inc. touch this sign every day as they leave to work their nefarious plans. They pursue this motto at all costs, to subvert and sabotage small businesses and their efforts to build better lives everywhere, the world over.

CHAOS Inc. is a privately held multinational corporation. Their reach is vast.

THE CREW

There are Seven Agents of Chaos, who you can think of as the board of directors of CHAOS Inc. They are reprehensible characters. As I describe them keep in mind that, while they're made up, these characters are based on *real-life* business phenomena. As fictional characters, I've taken a lot of care in making them as scary as possible.

THE CON acts as CEO of CHAOS Inc. He's the leader of the group. The irony of the Con is that he got you into the business in the first place. Even though entrepreneurship is a worthwhile endeavor, the Con distorts your perspective. He tells you that by sacrificing yourself on the altar of your business, by devoting time, effort, energy, and financial resources into growing your business, someday it will all pay off. This is the story you told yourself, right?

For a lot of entrepreneurs, that payoff keeps getting pushed further and further into the future.

Yet the Con goads you ever onward. He says, "It will be worth it *in the end*."

The second is **JACK-OF-ALL-TRADES**. Jack tells you that you should multitask because you can do everything yourself—that you're the best at everything in your business. Jack tells you if you hand something off, if you delegate, it will cause chaos because you're the only person fit to do the work of your business.

Jack-of-All-Trades tells you: "No one can do it as well as you." And, to a degree, he's right . . . which makes him all the more dangerous.

THE GORILLA is an employee who looks strong, who does a lot of things well, and who truly has a lot of strengths in your business. But he uses his strengths to divert attention from all of the messes he creates. The Gorilla essentially holds your business hostage.

The Gorilla is the employee that you think about late at night, asking yourself, "How do I get rid of him?" Yet, right before you fall asleep, another thought crosses your mind: "I can't get rid of the Gorilla because I need him."

You're not a malicious person; yet occasionally, during your fitful sleep, you dream of your Gorilla getting hit by a truck on his way to work tomorrow.

MS. OPPORTUNITY is the Con's baby sister, and she's responsible for distracting you. She convinces you to chase different opportunities that look profitable because hey, there's money over there!

Ms. Opportunity says, "I know you're good at what you do. You're awesome at it. You're so good at it, you would be good at other things, like this right here. So shiny, isn't it? So lustrous. Do you feel the weight of it? You could totally make money doing this, you big stud. Try it. You'll see. You're going to make so much money and be so gosh darn happy just as soon as you put that first thing down and try some of this right here."

Ms. Opportunity distracts you from the core of your business. She's the Kansas City Shuffle at CHAOS Inc. She's a master of three-card monte. Now you see it, now you . . .

SIPHON takes the form of customers, but the kind you would rather avoid. Siphon-customers make absurd requests that bleed you dry. They don't want to see you make money. Sometimes you wonder if these customers want your service or your constant, unwavering attention. These customers have weaponized the phrase: "The customer is always right." They use it on your business the same way robbers use ski masks and baseball bats.

Siphon is a customer who takes far more from your business than she will ever give back.

THE JUMBLER is the Chief Marketing Officer for CHAOS Inc. He turns your marketing plan into a perpetual gamble, where you throw things at the wall, hoping they stick, hoping in your wildest dreams to hit the jackpot. Postcards or Facebook? Print vs. Online. Should we use the headline our receptionist wrote during lunch or hire a writer? What should our website say about us? Is that guy selling space ads for the local business magazine full of crap? How can I tell?

The Jumbler makes you think goodwill and hope constitute a marketing strategy.

OVERLOAD is the last villain. Overload is short for Information Overload. Her primary weapon is data—piles of it. Entrepreneurs know that knowledge is power. More information means more knowledge, right? Wrong. Dead wrong. There's a reason "information" and "knowledge" are two separate and distinct words. It's because they're two different things.

The symptom of Overload's special brand of chaos is Analysis Paralysis. She gets you searching, ever searching, for just one right answer.

Now we've exposed the rogues' gallery of CHAOS Inc. Odds are, as I've described them, you've winced in pain at a few of these villainous characters. You know they've got you squarely in their sights, and you've been losing the battle.

Wouldn't it be nice if someone like Superman came down from the sky and vanquished all of these villains for you, like in a comic book? Or maybe the government could pass a law, making CHAOS Inc. and all of its sister companies illegal. This sounds like a job for Batman, right?

There is hope, my friend. Read on and see . . .

ACTION PLAN

Based on what you learned in this chapter, what is one action step you will take?

ACTION FOR CHAPTER 1:

_____

_____

CHAPTER 2

THE FOCUSED BUSINESS MODEL

THE HERO

Let's face it, no business superhero is going to sweep down from the sky and rescue you. Heck, there's not even a Daddy Warbucks to rescue your little orphan fanny.

No, it's YOUR job to banish these ne'er-do-wells from your business. You are the hero of this story.

As the CEO, President, Founder, and Owner, you are the only person with the power to affect real change. Your resourcefulness is what got you started in business in the first place. A gift was not magically bestowed upon you from the heavens. You weren't bit by a spider. You didn't take a pill or drink a magic potion. You did not get into business for any crazy, supernatural reason. You got into business and succeeded so far because of your resources, your ingenuity, and your ability to make connections.

THE PLAN

The solution to chaos depends upon you, yet first, you must understand the big picture. Before you can begin applying focus tools, you'll need to buy into what I call the **FOCUSED BUSINESS MODEL**. Think of it as one, unifying business plan for every successful business. It consists of three steps:

- First, **FOCUS** on one area of your business

- Second, hone that area of focus to perfection until you achieve **MASTERY**

- Third, then— and only then—begin the process of **DIVERSIFICATION**

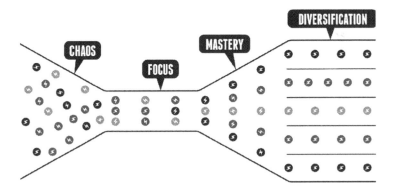

The first step is **FOCUS**. What is focus? Remember my definition of Chaos? Focus is eerily similar, with just a two-word change.

Focus, as I define it, is

THE *STRATEGIC* ALLOCATION OF RESOURCES TOWARD THAT WHICH IS OF *MOST* VALUE.

Focus is like chaos, except we trade "haphazard" for "strategic" resource allocation, and we trade "variable value" for "most value."

My job is to help you discover that which is of most value, then strategically apply your resources toward making your business more fun and more profitable. Then you can achieve mastery.

How do I define mastery? I believe entrepreneurs have mastered a business when it runs **PREDICTABLY** and **AUTOMATICALLY**. It will never be 100 percent predictable because, well, things happen. But business mastery means that, barring acts of God, everything happens as if your console is set to autopilot. It's that point when you don't even have to show up. You've mastered your business when you're making money while you sleep.

But let's return to the Focused Business Model for a moment. What examples do we have that can show it in action? As a superhero, you need a super model, right? And I know just the super model for you . . .

THE SUPER MODEL

Believe it or not, Tyra Banks is a perfect example of someone whose career followed the Focused Business Model.

Wait? Tyra Banks? The host of *America's Next Top Model*? Supermodels don't do anything but stand around, posing for pictures, right? Do I need to get my head checked? Am I going crazy? Is this a good example?

Yes. It is. It's an awesome example. Open your mind, and try to keep up.

Tyra Banks started out as a model. She mastered the business of being a model before she became a household name, which she also mastered before she became an

- Author

- Entrepreneur

- Talk show host

- Actor

- TV producer

- Harvard graduate

- Musician

- Charity founder

- And a lot of other things!

What would have happened if Tyra Banks tried to do all of these things at the same time? Do you think she would have been anywhere near as successful? If she had tried to do all of those things at the same time, where would she be today?

In my experience, most entrepreneurs know the answer to this question . . . instantly. Why? Because that is their day-to-day existence! It's the world they are living in right now: near perpetual chaos!

You cannot do everything at the same time and expect to succeed. What Tyra is teaching people to do now, with *America's Next Top Model*, she mastered first. She focused on being a model, became a supermodel, and then diversified into everything else.

MASTERY IN ONE FIELD LEADS TO OPPORTUNITY IN OTHER FIELDS. That is the final step of the Focused Business Model: mastery leads to diversification. Focus, Mastery, and—then and only then— Diversification.

Diversification never leads to mastery in all areas. There's too much to do to master everything at the same time.

Yet diversification first, or at least too early, is where most small entrepreneurs begin. And that is the Chaotic Business Model.

OTHER FAMOUS EXAMPLES

Not convinced yet? Not liking the Tyra example? Consider a few more . . .

OPRAH WINFREY mastered TV and radio first, then got into everything else: acting, her talk show, her book club, the O Network, and on and on. Focus, Mastery, Diversification.

ARNOLD SCHWARZENEGGER is an interesting case. He started by bodybuilding, then built a successful business, transitioned into acting, and became governor of California. Focus, Mastery, Diversification.

MICHAEL SYMON began with perfecting the craft of cooking. Now he owns multiple businesses and is an international TV star. Focus, Mastery, Diversification.

And of course, I can't forget my most dangerous fan, **CHUCK NORRIS**.[2] His mastery of martial arts led to acting, which led to businesses, infomercials, charitable work, and now . . . well, world domination. Focus, Mastery, Diversification, Chucktatorship.

I'm sure you've already thought of many, many more. Take almost any individual mega-success and you will see the Focused Business Model in action . . . over and over.

But what do most entrepreneurs do instead? They follow the Chaos Model! Maybe a little focus, then lots of diversification, and back to chaos. Rinse and repeat.

BUSINESSES DO IT, TOO

Let's move away from these individual examples for a moment. In reality, most of you are trying to build a business, not a celebrity, right? So let's consider a few business-based examples of the Focused Business Model.

Tony Hsieh and **ZAPPOS.COM** sold shoes for seven years before they diversified into all of the product lines they offer today. Zappos is a huge success, both in running a successful business and in creating an awesome workplace culture. When Tony Hsieh went into the market with his business partners, they looked at all the different things they could do, and they saw an opportunity in selling shoes online. Then they mastered it. Now, Zappos is mastering the art of selling *every* kind of apparel on the Internet. Focus, Mastery, Diversification.

---

2.   Chuck actually referenced me and my book, *The Myth of Multitasking*, in *The Official Chuck Norris Fact Book*. You'll find it under the fact, "Chuck Norris can kill two stones with one bird." Seriously.

How about **OTTERBOX**, founded by Curt Richardson? This company with now over a half billion in sales began humbly in the early 1990s with a prototype waterproof box. It honed this product for several years and then later evolved into the mobile device market, starting with the iPod. Now it provides cases for every popular mobile device and has even expanded into custom case design for enterprise and government use. Focus, Mastery, Diversification.

Then there is **PLUM ORGANICS** based in Emeryville, California. Plum focused initially on the organic baby food market, developing the highest-quality and most-respected option on the market. Then, once CEO Neil Grimmer helped the company establish dominance in that new niche, they began to expand their offerings into healthy kids' snacks, meals, and more. Focus, Mastery, Diversification.

ADEN & ANAIS, founded by Raegan Moya-Jones, began by sharing a simple Australian tradition: muslin swaddling wraps for babies. They have since become a worldwide phenomenon with a variety of muslin-based products. Focus, Mastery, Diversification.

Anisa Telwar founded **ANISA INTERNATIONAL** in 1992. For over ten years she and her company focused on the marketing and distribution of cosmetic products. In 2003 Anisa began the diversification process into manufacturing and developing products. Anisa's twenty-year story arc has been one of repeated Focus, Mastery, Diversification.

Over time, the results from businesses that follow this model become more dramatic.

GOOGLE started out as a search engine. What *don't* they do now? Focus, Mastery, Diversification.

MARRIOTT began as a little restaurant and stayed that way for many years until the first hotel opened. Focus, Mastery, Diversification.

AMAZON.COM used to sell nothing but books. Focus, Mastery, Diversification.

Got it? Now it's time for you to take ownership of this concept. Take a brief moment and list **THREE** other examples of the Focused Business Model.

1. _____

2. _____

3. _____

An Example Close to Home

Allow me to get personal for a moment. **LARRY H. MILLER** was a positive influence in my life as an entrepreneur. He also happened to be an icon of business in the Rocky Mountain area, particularly Utah.

Larry was one of my teachers at the Marriott School of Management. Every Tuesday, from 1:30 to 4:30 p.m., he came to the classroom to talk about business. We could ask him any question we wanted to, and he would respond candidly.

But Larry didn't simply answer whatever questions the class threw at him. He would tell stories, most of them about his life and entrepreneurial experience.

Larry had a gift for numbers. He was good at memorizing numbers and recognizing patterns.

Larry turned his talent for numbers into fortunes by memorizing Toyota car parts. He memorized the part numbers and started noticing patterns pertaining to the source of particular parts. After noticing locking gas caps only came from two manufacturers, he approached his boss at the Toyota dealership about buying the entire supply and becoming the source. In essence, Larry told his boss, "If you give me one million, we'll turn it into two million in a month." They did, and the rest is history.

Larry started with car parts and ended up buying the majority of car dealerships in the Salt Lake area. From there he purchased the Utah Jazz. Then he started Utah's Megaplex Movie Theater chain. Larry passed away recently, yet left a business legacy that will live for decades.

Focus leads to mastery leads to diversification.

Got it? Good.

Now let's begin assembling the tools you'll need to fight CHAOS Inc. and stay true to the Focused Business Model!

ACTION PLAN

Based on what you learned in this chapter, what is one action step you will take?

ACTION FOR CHAPTER 2:

_____

_____

CHAPTER 3

YOU VS. THE CON

et's meet the Chief Executive Officer of CHAOS Inc.—the Con. His power and gift as an agent of chaos is exactly what you would expect: deception.

How does the Con con you?

He tells you things like you are going to get stinking, bloody, rotten rich. He tells you someday you will have all the time in the world to collect and restore old Porsches, or race airplanes, or own your own pro football team, or buy a house in the Hamptons, or live abroad for the rest of your life—worry free.

Consider your business dream—that imaginary destination you fantasize about occasionally. Can you see it? That dream is the lie the Con told you that got you into business in the first place. I say the Con told you that lie because it softens the blow a bit. In reality, though, *you* told *yourself* that lie.

Written down like that, in all of its blunt accuracy, it is the most depressing thing in the world. You conned yourself into this crazy life of entrepreneurship, hoping for happy families, buckets of money to donate to charities, private planes, beautiful people, and freedom. Or something like that, right? Yet, if you're like most entrepreneurs, you are a hot mess. It's nothing like what you dreamed about in the beginning.

LIES THE CON TELLS YOU

People are conned by all kinds of crazy things . . . things like the kind of world domination that is marked by owning your own island and your own NASCAR team. The Con's most devastating trick is how he convinces you that only big rewards have value. He tells you the longer you pile up your time and effort, eventually you'll be able to reward yourself with the blessings of your business.

The Con's lies convince you to put off enjoying the fruits of your labor, your dreams manifested in real life, until *later*.

The Con's favorite saying is, "It will be worth it in the end." He tells you it is okay to work eighty hours a week because it will be worth it in the end. It is okay to take time away from your family because you are giving your family the things you went without as a youngster. It is worth all the expense and leveraging your credit rating to the max because you are going to become a millionaire over and over again just as soon as someone comes in and buys your business right out from under your feet.

What about the consequences of believing the Con? What does that look like?

Depression is one consequence. So is the loss of motivation, which can absolutely kill a business. As a business coach I have seen the road to the Con's big lie littered with failed marriages, wrecked health, mental illness, and, ironically, poverty.

The consequences of believing the Con can truly be life threatening. Larry H. Miller, who I mentioned in the prologue, is one such example. Despite doing a lot of good, Larry, in a very real way, killed himself physically. He continually worked himself to exhaustion in a way that took an irreversible toll on his body.

Believe the Con and you might as well be shooting heroin. Entrepreneurship has the potential to be just as unhealthy.

COLLATERAL DAMAGE

It is also easy to con yourself out of your family life. I've learned that a major by-product of my work to help entrepreneurs has been to help bring families closer together.

The Con would tell you that you can spend months away from your family or your friends or your hobbies and then make it all up in large chunks spent with them later. This is a damnable lie.

First, you rarely truly make good on those promises made to yourself and others. Second, real life does not work that way. There are some moments that can never be reclaimed. Our children only have one first step. They will only perform in the *Nutcracker* as a seven-year-old once. Your spouse will only be excited to go on that date you promised to go on once. Your friend's birthday party happens only once. Sure, there will be other wonderful times, but not any time exactly like that *one* magic moment.

By choice, I have always been there for my kids. I do not work weekends and I stop work at 5:00 p.m. every day. That means no calls, voice mails, e-mails, projects, or anything work-related.

Why?

Part of the reason is that I grew up as a "latchkey kid," for lack of a better term. My parents got divorced when I was very young. I did not see my father as much as I would have liked to have seen him. My mom needed to work a lot, so I was dropped off at other people's homes in the morning, stayed at other people's homes in the afternoon, and then finally came home, trying to figure out which set of family rules I was now expected to live by. When I got older and moved into a new area, my mom literally paid a kid from the neighborhood to come over and be my friend when I got home from school. True story.

Does any of this sound familiar? It is a common enough story, one too many of us have lived through. Because of my past, I made conscious decisions to be there for my kids.

But there is an even more compelling reason why I focus on family. It comes from the experiences I've heard from countless entrepreneurs just like you. I've heard your regret.

What I hear are the voices that say, "My son turned twelve, and I realize I haven't watched him grow up." "I should have spent more time with my wife." "I could have been involved more." That is the voice I hear. It is the entrepreneur's voice. It is the voice of a lot of other working people, too. It is a cost, a dear price, far too many of us, and our loved ones, pay.

CAUGHT UP IN IT ALL

Time goes by so fast, doesn't it? It can be very difficult, in the milieu of running a business, in the firefight of sales and competition, to know exactly how fast time is passing, how much you stand to miss. It is very easy to miss your family's most important moments because you are busy running a business, trying to give them everything you *think* they want.

Yet, more often than not, what your family wants is *you*.

They couldn't care less about you becoming the hero of your business. Your family wants you to be their hero, and they deserve that more than anything else from you.

The Con tells you that you can have one or the other—your family or your business—but never both at the same time. In order to be your kids' hero, you have to first become the hero of your business. These are the things the Con whispers to you, across the table, when you are having your fourth late-night take-out dinner of the week with him.

Even if you manage to escape the Con for a couple nights a week, you are not present for your family if you are constantly checking your phone for new e-mails. Yes, you may make it home by 5 p.m., but you are not *present* for them. Keep this up and when your kids get older, they'll become conditioned to your absence. It is not as though they'll suddenly want to see more of you when they are teenagers!

Yet the Con tells you to *wait* to spend time with your kids. We follow his advice, then wonder why young adults get into so much trouble.

Businesses, left unchecked, have the power to destroy marriages, too. I have worked with a lot of husband and wife teams over the years. Regardless of whether you run the business together or your better half stays home with your family, business wreaks its own special kind of havoc on marriages.

The same devastating effects of chaos can be found in destroyed friendships or discarded hobbies and personal interests. The Con wants you to believe these things will *always* be there for you. But the longer they are left untended the more they atrophy and, eventually, wither and die.

It comes down to this: there are more important things in life than work. Time is irreplaceable. It is the rarest and most valuable commodity on earth. We must spend it wisely.

You do not have to fall for the Con's shtick to be successful. You can spend more time with your family, and there is no need to wait.

Ultimate-ly Exhausting

First, let's talk about *business harvest*. My definition:

Business Harvest: Any moment where you *enjoy* the fruits of your entrepreneurial labors, to any degree

---

This is a radically different definition than what you'll read about in standard entrepreneurial fare. When most entrepreneurs, venture capitalists, and associated media think of harvest, they think of it only one way: an *Ultimate* Harvest.

The Ultimate Harvest is that point off in the future where business owners and investors, in some form, cash out. Perhaps they sell, they hand the business off to someone else to manage, they franchise or make a public stock offering.

However you define it, Ultimate Harvest is the goal that drives the business leader forward day in and day out. They believe that then, and only then, are they finally able to enjoy all the fruits of their labors, their hard work, the risks that they've put in the business.

The Ultimate Harvest is, indeed, a good thing. It's something you should be working toward. However, the Cons want your focus to stay on this distant destination and *nothing* else. Why?

Because when he can get you to put off enjoying just a little bit of the fruits of your entrepreneurial labors as you go along, you'll likely become depressed, discouraged, and burnt-out. The Con will keep whipping your rear end like a slave master, over and over, and at the same time he keeps moving the finish line farther and farther away.

It's a bit like the classic illustration of the donkey chasing the carrot.

Pop quiz: Can you guess who the real ass in this picture is?

Let's be clear. The Ultimate Harvest is not the Con's con. Quite the contrary, your dream of that harvest is a good thing. The "con" part of the Con's shtick is that the Ultimate Harvest is the *only* thing that matters and everything must be sacrificed to achieve it.

Focus Tool: Harvest Strategy

But you do not have to wait! You can create many *mini-harvests*.

Remember my previous definition of business harvest? *Any* moment can count. Therefore, mini-harvests are planned, bite-sized moments to stop and enjoy what you're doing, no matter how small. These small harvests require relatively little in the way of capital and even time. In fact, they deliver a powerful ROI punch by keeping the most productive employee in the business—you—continually motivated.

By having lots of planned mini-harvests along your journey toward Ultimate Harvest, you'll actually stay more motivated and rewarded. Even more, you'll be able to avoid that painful and unnecessary damage caused to yourself and others that I mentioned earlier.

This combination of mini-harvests and Ultimate Harvest is what I like to call your Harvest Strategy. This is the first of the seven focus tools that you will use to defeat CHAOS Inc.

First, let's talk about mini-harvests, which come in four delicious flavors.

DAILY–The daily harvest is a bit of an oasis in the midst of the rush of your day. Daily mini-harvests typically last between five minutes to one hour. How might you take a break from all the work that's going along? What activity would help you relax and refresh your mind and body? Perhaps you go for a walk or listen to music or even take a nap. This small bit of reward, done consistently, will yield big dividends in the long run.

WEEKLY–Weekly harvests often revolve around hobbies. It's shocking to me how often I ask my clients, "What do you do for fun?" and they draw a blank. Many entrepreneurs work so hard day in and day out that they've forgotten how to have fun. What would be a fun activity to engage in weekly? What hobbies have you neglected . . . or always wanted to take up but never gave yourself the permission to do so?

MONTHLY–The monthly harvest is a chance to step away from the business mentally. It's a larger moment, perhaps a full weekend, where you can take a rest and then come back renewed for the coming month. Many entrepreneurs I've worked with take an extended vacation monthly, visit the spa, or just check themselves out of the business for one full day.

YEARLY–The yearly harvest is the biggest of the mini-harvests. It's one event or reward per year where you celebrate the successes of the previous year. Perhaps it's a big vacation with friends and family. Perhaps it's a large investment in some hobby that you love and enjoy. The choice is yours. Having that yearly target to work toward will help motivate you throughout the rest of the year.

Take a moment now and complete this very simple form I've provided for you. Jot down some of your thoughts about what you might do for each of these mini-harvests.

DAILY	WEEKLY	MONTHLY	YEARLY
yoga, Happy Hour	*date night, singing*	*3 day weekend, entertaining*	*Reno, vacation*

Need some ideas? Here are some of the mini-harvests my clients past and present have enjoyed:

- **DAILY**

  Taking a walk, listening to music, enjoying a nice lunch, watching TV, exercising

- ### WEEKLY

  Riding motorcycles, volunteering at school, coaching, date with spouse, half-day off

- ### MONTHLY

  Charitable event, three-day weekend with spouse, day at the spa, date-day with children

- ### YEARLY

  One extended vacation, company trip, major purchase, finishing basement

PERSONAL VS. FAMILY HARVEST

That's a good start. We have a bit more to consider when it comes to your harvest strategy: balance. We tend to put either ourselves or our family first.

Some entrepreneurs, like the get-rich-quick-and-sell-out guys, put themselves before their families. As you know, that strategy often ends in personal disaster. Consistently neglect those closest to you and, like Scrooge in the classic tale of *A Christmas Carol*, you may find that your success is hollow. Mankind, especially those closest to you, is your business.

However, I've found that many of my clients have the opposite tendency, which is to put their families before themselves. That also creates imbalance, opening the doorway to lose yourself and your business, all at the same time. Many of us who got into business to "have more time with our families" fall into this trap. You must create a harvest for yourself; otherwise the harvest for your family will not matter nearly as much.

There is a healthy balance here, and it's easy to create.

Consider this second version of the mini-harvest chart below. This time, you'll notice that there is a second row to distinguish between personal and family. If you feel the "family" term doesn't completely describe your social status, think of that row as "friends" or "loved ones" instead.

Now copy the notes you made previously about your harvest strategy. As you do so, put mini-harvest ideas into their correct category. For instance, if you said you would go on a weekly date with your wife, I believe that belongs in the "Family" row of the weekly column. If you said you wanted to exercise thirty minutes each day, odds are that is a "Personal" item.

	DAILY	WEEKLY	MONTHLY	YEARLY
PERSONAL	yoga run	singing	3 day weekend	special couples spa
FAMILY	happy hour	date night	entertain	vacation Rens

After you do this, you'll notice which mini-harvests for either Personal or Family are left blank. Now, take a moment and consider activities or rewards you could use to fill in the blanks.

WHAT ABOUT THE ULTIMATE?

We've covered the mini-harvest, but you may have noticed I've said nothing about determining your Ultimate Harvest. That isn't because it's not unimportant. It is—critically important—to define the endgame of your business. However, I won't spend too much time discussing the Ultimate Harvest in this book. Why?

In my experience, many entrepreneurs already have this harvest defined. They've been listening to the Con's whisperings so long that they're already painfully obsessed with the idea. Also, an in-depth discussion on the numerous possibilities of how to ultimately harvest your business would, well, fill another book. And finally, often what you believe to be the final destination ends up shifting, sometimes dramatically. So much can and will change in your business that what you believe today to be your Ultimate Harvest will manifest completely different than expected.

However, to help you define your Ultimate Harvest I'd like you to consider some questions I might ask you if you were my coaching client:

1. **WHAT DO YOU WANT?** Imagine a magic genie told you he could make any result happen for your business. What would you wish for? Do you want to sell the business? Do you want to hand it off to someone else to run while you reap the benefits? Write down a few notes about your answer.

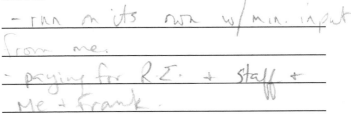

2. **WHAT BENEFIT DO YOU GET FROM THAT RESULT? WHAT BENEFIT DOES YOUR FAMILY GET FROM THAT RESULT?** There are many motives for taking your business to Ultimate Harvest. The more meaningful the motive is to you, the more successful you'll be. Also, in the interest of balance, make sure that you consider both the rewards for yourself and the rewards for your loved ones. Jot down a few notes about these benefits here:

BENEFIT TO ME:

- time to relax + enjoy life
- train, pursue other interests
- fly - breed dogs - music -
- garden, yoga, cook

BENEFIT TO MY FAMILY:

- freedom - more time together
- less stress + fatigue - travel.

3. **WHEN DO YOU WANT TO ACCOMPLISH THIS?** The "when" question is critical because it has everything to do with time, money, and risk. If the "when" is short-term, that means you're going to have to expend a lot of time on a weekly basis working to get there. You'll need a lot more money, most likely other people's money. Third, the shorter the

time line, the higher the risk that you will not succeed in reaching that Ultimate Harvest.

If, on the other hand, your Ultimate Harvest is several years into the future, then that allows you to work more reasonable hours. You can bootstrap and use your own money to get there. The risk of failure is lower.

The choice is yours, though. Make a few notes about the "when" of your Ultimate Harvest:

by the time I am 50 I would like to be supported by business 2021 + have all located in own bldg. w/ all R.E. cash flow+

4. **SUM IT UP.** Now, combine the notes from above and make a single paragraph that defines what you want, what you're going to get from it, and how soon you want it.

By the year 2012 I + my family will be supported by my business. I will spend less than 6 hours per week on business activities + will have time to relax, exercise + pursue my hobbies + They will also allow me to spend time w family + friends + for Frank to be free from his

The paragraph you created above forms the foundation for your Ultimate Harvest strategy. As I mentioned, this may evolve over time, but just knowing where you want to go is a step toward stopping the Con from continually moving the carrot away from you. There is a destination on this crazy train ride of entrepreneurship.

Locking Up the Con

With the Harvest Strategy, you now have the tool you need to thwart the Con.

When he tells you to keep pushing, keep driving toward an ever-shifting Ultimate Harvest, you can tell him to get lost. Instead, think about and look forward to your next weekly or monthly mini-harvest.

When he whispers in your ear that "it will be worth it in the end," you can tell him it's worth it TODAY. It's worth it today because you're going to take a break, or spend time with your child, or any number of other worthwhile mini-harvests you choose.

The first and perhaps most powerful of the seven Agents of Chaos is now subdued underneath your feet. No longer will the CEO of CHAOS Inc. be able to sway your attention so easily.

Now you're ready to tackle the next agent: the Jack-of-All-Trades.

ACTION PLAN

Based on what you learned in this chapter, what is one action step you will take?

ACTION FOR CHAPTER 3:

<u>Plot a course each day</u>
<u>and celebrate small goals.</u>

CHAPTER 4

YOU VS. JACK-OF-ALL-TRADES

You'd Better Know Jack

The next agent is CHAOS Inc.'s Chief Operating Officer, Jack-of-All-Trades.

Jack loves it when you multitask. He wants you to waste time switching from task to task to task to task—as often as possible. This is how he keeps you away from your true strengths.

Delegation is a fine art, one worth mastering, yet most entrepreneurs run madly in the other direction, trying to do everything themselves instead. When you're having another one of those late-night take-out meals with Jack-of-

All-Trades, he tells you point blank that "nobody can do it as well as you can."

They can't, can they? They're not like you. They're not as hard-charging or as hardworking as you are.

Sounds reasonable, but it's a lie. First, there are numerous tools and apps in existence that can free up truckloads of time if you commit to learning how to use them. Yet, you're so starved when it comes to time that you hesitate to *take* time to embrace things that would *make* you time. It's the proverbial catch-22—but of your own making.

Second, your employees can do many things better than you can. All it takes is a little systems documentation and a little accountability. Yet, you're an entrepreneur. You do a lot of things well. You decided a long time ago that you can do whatever you set your mind to doing. You have proven yourself right, time and time again. And, of course, Jack reminds you of all that.

If you built your business from the time it was a newborn, it was probably your ability to do ten or fifteen things well that got your business off the ground in the first place. At one time, wearing many hats saved you money.

Once your business gets off the ground, though, chaos overtakes you. Jack-of-All-Trades keeps you pinned down by spreading you in twenty different directions.

Face it, there are a bunch of things you have no business doing at your business.

Bookkeeping. Taxes. Administrative work. Going to the store. Running errands. Buying pens and pencils. Invoicing. Replacing toner cartridges. On and on. Nobody does it as well as you can.

Or do they? I guarantee you any sixteen-year-old can go to the store and buy pens just as well as you can. So why do *you* do it?

Because Jack-of-All-Trades wants to put as much distance as humanly possible between you and your MVP—your Most Valuable Position in the company. Jack wants you to concentrate on your LVPs—your Least Valuable Positions.

And this makes Jack-of-All-Trades the dark horse at CHAOS Inc.—their secret weapon.

THE COST

More than anything else, Jack robs you of your time. He wants you to waste time, and time is always more valuable than money because you can never get it back once you spend it. At least with money you can always make more. This isn't true for time. Time is irreplaceable and thus invaluable.

The time-cost spills beyond your business, too. Jack supports the mission of the Con by ravaging your family life. Doing more things at the same time increases your stress levels. It also takes time away from more important things, like cultivating personal relationships and spending quality time with your family. Each and every task takes longer when you multitask. As I illustrated in depth in my book *The Myth of Multitasking*, the more you switchtask, the longer everything takes.

Doing everything yourself also makes it extremely hard to grow your business because there is a ceiling to the time one person can spend doing something. All by yourself, your business can only go so far. Let's think about why this is true.

Just for a moment, let's imagine Jack-of-All-Trades is correct. Nobody can do it as well as you can, and you truly are the very best at everything at your business. Maybe that's true. It very well could be true. Let's have a look at why you *want* it to be false.

There are 168 hours in a week, and you can do whatever you want with them to an extent. All by itself, sleep takes thirty to forty hours out of your week, leaving you with about 128 hours to spend doing what you need to do. You have to eat. Nature calls. These are the basics. Once you account for the basics—sleeping, eating, and "personal" time—you have one hundred hours left. One hundred hours, max.

Do you enjoy working hundred-hour weeks?

Even if you do—you twisted person, you—your business can only grow so much with you working on it *only* one hundred hours a week.

"*Only* one hundred hours? I'm working my tail off!" you say.

I say, "So what?"

BLUE SKY BLUES

Consider *blue sky*. Blue sky is everything in the business that has no real value to a potential buyer. In your case, that's anything that can't be sold or can be *attributed directly to the work hours of the business owner*. Your business needs more than blue sky to be truly successful. Without work that is taking place *independent of you*, you're building zero equity in your business.

And what happens when the time comes to sell your business? You will have cheated yourself out of your harvest with a blue-sky business, a business that exists solely based on what the owner brings to it. You have nothing but blue sky to sell, and, unless you get lucky, nobody on earth is going to buy it from you.

You'll then realize blue sky is summed up by its initials . . . BS.

In short, you built a job, not a business. And it was a pretty miserable job at that because it demanded long hours for little return!

Like the Con, Jack wants to cheat you out of your harvest. Jack steals as much time from you as he possibly can, tricks you into thinking you're the best man for every job, and *then* cheats you out of a harvest for all your effort. How evil is that?

Every time you insist on doing it yourself and not looking for shortcuts, such as apps and tools, you're robbing yourself of time and equity. You're ignoring the hard work that others *have already done* to make your life easier and more successful. Jack wins.

Every time you put yourself in the middle of an employee's task and micromanage, you're telling them you don't trust them to do it right. You're questioning their skills. You're doing them a great disservice. Ultimately, you're doing their work for them. Jack wins again.

But it doesn't have to be this way. You can beat Jack-of-All-Trades at his own game.

THE TRUTH

Let's take a moment and figure out exactly *what* you are doing in your business. Yes, you know it's a lot, but how much—really? I've found that helping people see the truth will change behavior faster than telling them what they're doing wrong. So let's take a good, hard look at the truth together.

On the next page, I've provided a very simple checklist. It contains a list of all the many possible positions I've found entrepreneurs might have in a given week.

It's simple to use this worksheet.[3] Just put a check mark next to each position you believe you fill, to any degree, in an average workweek.

☑	POSITION	DESCRIPTION	EST. VALUE
☑	Founder	Provides vision, inspiration, creation of entire businesses	HIGH
☑	President	Acts as figurehead, motivation of company as a whole	HIGH
☐	CEO or COO	Provides overall operations management, execution of vision	HIGH-MED
☐	Marketing Manager	Develops, manages, and oversees marketing campaigns	MEDIUM
☐	Sales Executive	Creates big-ticket lead generation and sales conversion	HIGH-MED
☐	Sales Representative	Provides one-on-one low-level lead generation and sales conversion	MEDIUM
☑	Mid-level Manager (Titles vary)	Oversees success (may manage multiple groups)	MED-LOW
☑	Copywriter	Delivers sales material copywriting, including emails, brochures, ads	MEDIUM
☑	Editor or Beta Tester	Tests materials, products, websites for flaws and submits recommendations for improvement	MED-LOW
☐	Office Manager	Manages the behind the scenes office details	MED-LOW
☐	Graphic Designer	Creates the visual materials of the business	MED-LOW
☐	R&D Manager	Develops and tests new products and services	HIGH-MED
☐	Legal Counsel	Deals with minor, day-to-day legal issues and questions	HIGH-MED
☑	Project Manager	Coordinates the calendar and work of several people on a per-project basis (including events)	MEDIUM

---

3. Want a clean copy you can download and print out?
Visit FocusedBusiness.com/mvp . We've got one ready for you!

☑	POSITION	DESCRIPTION	EST. VALUE
☑	Customer Support	Answers the most basic questions of customers	LOW
☑	Customer Loyalty Manager	Provides higher-end customer support and develops strategies for customer retention	MEDIUM
☐	Public Relations Specialist	Responds to media inquiries, coordinates appearances for president	MEDIUM
☑	Technician (Titles vary)	The person who delivers or creates the core product or service of the company	MED-LOW
☑	Receptionist	Frontline answering of phones with no sales role	LOW
☑	Webmaster	Develops websites and back-end programming; executes vision of graphic designer	MED-LOW
☑	Administrative Assistant	Clerical work, errand running	LOW
☑	Janitor	Everyday cleaning	LOW
☐	Maintenance Specialist	Repairing everyday equipment	MED-LOW
☑	Bookkeeper	Enters financial data and may provide low-level reporting	MED-LOW
☐	A/R or Collections Specialist	Follows up on past due accounts and collects money	MED-LOW
☑	Accountant or Controller	Files returns, generates reports, pays bills and provides occasional financial feedback	MEDIUM
☑	IT Manager	Sets up company information technology-strategy and troubleshoots computer or network issues	MEDIUM
☐	"Create Your Own Title"	This list is by no means exhaustive. Create titles for any other mini-positions you fill and estimate their value.	VARIES

After you complete this worksheet, take a moment to step back and look at it objectively. What do you notice about your positions?

There are a whole bunch of them, right? How many did you check? Three? Thirteen? Thirty?

How much of the "dirty work" are you doing? I've been watching a lot of movies lately, and I noticed gangsters don't execute their own hits. They hire people to do that. How long do you think crime bosses would last if they didn't? Probably about as long as most hit men. A sobering thought, right?

It's the same when you spread yourself all over the place and wear too many hats. You not only lower the life expectancy of your business, but your own as well.

So, let's stop this madness by turning Jack's approach on its head. Let's focus. Let's get strategic and remove everything that you're doing that isn't Most Valuable.

YOUR MVP

We're now going to identify your MVP. No, this isn't a sports hero or a top employee. Your MVP is your Most Valuable Position, the one or two positions that are most valuable to your business and your own well-being.

On the next page is the MVP worksheet[4], where you will list all of the positions you checkmarked on the Common Positions worksheet. That's step one, so go ahead and do that now.

---

4.   Also available for free download at FocusedBusiness.com/mvp. Awesome.

POSITION	EST. VALUE (LOW, MED, HIGH)	YOUR ABILITY (-,=,+)
FOUNDER PRESIDENT	High	+
CEO	High-Med	+
Marketing Mgr.	Med	−
Mid level Mgr.	Med-Low	−
Copywriter	Med	=
Editor / Tester	Med-Low	−
Ofc Mgr	Med-Low	+
R + D Mgr	Med-high	+
Legal Counsel	Med-High	−
Project Manager	Med?	−
Customer Loyalty Mgr	Med	−
Technician	Med-low	+
Receptionist	low	−
Admin Assistant	low	−
Janitor	low	−
Bookkeeper	Med-low	=
Controller / Acct.	Med	−
IT Mgr.	Med	=

Also available for free download at FocusedBusiness.com/mvp.

				DATE		

$ / HR (Year Salary / 2040)	LOVE (Yes, No, Maybe)	RANK	CURRENT % (Avg. Week)	TARGET %	☑
	yes.	1	5	20	☑
	yes.	2	5	20	☑
	maybe	6	5	20	☑
	no	11	5	5	☑
	maybe	7	5	10	☑
	NO.	10	5	0	☑
	yes	4	5	5	☑
	no	15	5	0	☑
	no	9	5	0	☑
	maybe	5	5	10	☑
	no	8	10	5	☑
	no	18	10	5	☑
	no	16	5	0	☑
	no	17	5	0	☑
	no	12	5	0	☑
	no	13	5	0	☑
	no	14	5	0	☑
					☐
					☐
					☐
					☐
					☐

- After you list your positions, put the estimated value per hour in the next row: LOW, MEDIUM, or HIGH. I already gave you the answers in the Common Positions worksheet, so just transfer that information over.

- In the next column, give a rough estimate of your ability in this position with either a "-," "=," or "+" sign. Minus means you're below average. Equal means you're about average. Plus means you're above average.

- Next determine how much you just love filling that position. Running errands floats your boat? Put a "yes" there. If not, put a "no." Put "maybe" if you're really indecisive.

Now go through and rank all of these activities, using a "1" for your "top" position—the one that stands out in your mind based on your estimated value when doing it, your value per hour, and your love for it. Then, go ahead and rate the rest of the positions on down the line, using numbers "2" through "LOL!"

Don't get too analytical. That's what Overload would want you to do, darn her. Instead, just eyeball the answers you put in the previous rows. Then create a rank for all your positions. You'll end up having something that looks a bit like this:

TURN THE PAGE

POSITION	EST. VALUE (LOW, MED, HIGH)	YOUR ABILITY (-,=,+)
Founder	HIGH	=
Webmaster	MED	-
Bookkeeper	LOW	+
Marketing Manager	HIGH	=
Customer Support	LOW	+
Project Manager	MED	+

$ / HR (Year Salary / 2040)	LOVE (Yes, No, Maybe)	RANK	CURRENT % (Avg. Week)	TARGET %	☑
DATE			April 21	May 21	
$250	Yes	1			☐
$34	No	4			☐
$19	No	5			☐
$50	Yes	2			☐
$14	No	6			☐
$38	Maybe	3			☐
					☐
					☐
					☐
					☐
					☐
					☐
					☐
					☐
					☐

Your top two answers, rank 1 and rank 2, are now your MVPs. Congratulations! Now you know what you should *really* be doing with your time. Not fifty things. Just those two.

Sounds great, right? But not necessarily real life . . . yet. We need to take baby steps to get there.

That's where the last two columns come in: Current Percent and Target Percent. You're now going to set bite-sized goals that you can use to gradually bump up your total time on MVPs.

- First, put **TODAY'S DATE** above the Current Percent column. Then estimate the rough percentage you are spending on each position. Again, don't overanalyze it. Just make sure that the total between all the positions adds up to 100 percent.

- Second, put a date **THREE MONTHS FROM NOW** above the Target Percent column. This is the date by which you'll have made improvements in your time spent in MVPs. Create a **NEW, REALISTIC ESTIMATE** of how much time you want to be spending in these positions three months from now. HINT: the time spent in MVPs should go *up*, and the time spent in a few other positions should go *down*. Again, make sure the total adds up to 100 percent.

- Finally, if there is ANY difference between the Current Percent and the Target Percent column, place a check mark in the last column. This check mark is a big red flag shouting, "LOOK AT ME!" This indicates some action is required.

Your end result will look a little like this:

TURN THE PAGE
→

POSITION	EST. VALUE (LOW, MED, HIGH)	YOUR ABILITY (-,=,+)
Founder	HIGH	=
Webmaster	MED	-
Bookkeeper	LOW	+
Marketing Manager	HIGH	=
Customer Support	LOW	+
Project Manager	MED	+

$ / HR (Year Salary / 2040)	LOVE (Yes, No, Maybe)	RANK	DATE	April 21 CURRENT % (Avg. Week)	May 21 TARGET %	☑
$250	Yes	1		10	20	☑
$34	No	4		5	0	☑
$19	No	5		10	10	☐
$50	Yes	2		15	20	☑
$14	No	6		30	25	☑
$38	Maybe	3		30	25	☑
						☐
						☐
						☐
						☐
						☐
						☐
						☐
						☐
						☐

Now we know what your MVPs are. Your LVPs—Least Valuable Positions—are everything else. We also know where you want to make some changes to your schedule.

So, what's next? How do we make a real, meaningful change in your MVP time?

THE SHORT-TERM SOLUTION

A running joke between my wife and me is the phrase, "There's an app for that." This came about because one day I was teaching her how to think more like a geek. I told her that one thing all geeks know is that someone has likely already created an app for whatever you need done. Case in point: I found an app to help me manage the sub-in and sub-out of players on my son's flag football team. I'm still working on finding one that will deliver the snacks to hungry mouths right at the end of the game.

Well, in your case, the fastest way to off-load at least a few of your LVPs is to look for apps. This includes software programs. Internet-based software tools are especially helpful because they're so darn cost-effective.

Consider FreshBooks. This is a perfect example of an app that will save you mountains of time to reinvest into MVPs. In my case, I used to spend way too much time putting together expense reports and invoicing clients for my speaking gigs. Now, with just a snap of the camera and a few clicks, receipts are uploaded, invoices are created, and billing reminders are sent. Coupled with my Authorize.Net merchant account, FreshBooks even lets me instantly receive online payments.

The result? Hours saved, time reinvested in MVPs, my business grows, and Jack-of-All-Trades skulks away—defeated.

There are hundreds of apps, software programs, and websites out there that can help you do everything from getting fast, live transcription (Transcription Hub), to creating instant legal documents (LegalZoom.com), to getting top-drawer technical support (Experts Exchange).

If you forgive the generalization, I'd also lump business service providers in with business apps. For instance, OrangeSoda is an SEO company that helps small businesses dominate local search engine rankings. Jack wants you to do it yourself and learn all about SEO and keywords and Google algorithms and who-knows-what's-next. Pay an expert. Let them do it. Use the time you save to focus on your MVP, instead.

With just a little more effort, you can also outsource slightly bigger, but not-big-enough-for-a-full-time-employee, jobs using sites like oDesk. Yes, it takes a bit more setup time to find outsource partners, but the benefit gained far outweighs the small investment.

The point is, there's an app for that. Tell Jack to shut up . . . then go look for it.

THE LONG-TERM SOLUTION

Ultimately, as your business grows, you'll want to hire. You'll build more equity in your business if you have highly trained and accountable employees doing the work for you. Employees can use the apps I mentioned on your behalf, and much more. They can turn your business from a one-person MVP show to a thriving, focused business.

However, there is one, massive, hairy, ugly roadblock in the way of this solution. The Gorilla. Read on to learn how we can fight this Agent of Chaos together . . .

ACTION PLAN

Based on what you learned in this chapter, what is one action step you will take?

ACTION FOR CHAPTER 4:

off load my LUP's

CHAPTER 5

YOU VS. THE GORILLA

U p until now, the top brass at CHAOS Inc. have all been concepts. You know, not real people. So far they've been so powerful they haven't needed to show up in person because they exist in your own messed up business brain. Well there's another board member at CHAOS Inc. who works in the field, who actually shows up in person at your business. And no, we're not going to talk about those "friendly" salespeople who show up so often at your front door.

It's the Gorilla, and the Gorilla is a very interesting character. In all my years of coaching businesses, every single business I've ever worked with has had a

Gorilla. If the business has employees, it has a Gorilla, and the Gorilla is a real, living-and-breathing person.

The Gorilla is someone who works at your business, who makes you feel like you need him, and who may even bring a lot to the table, but ultimately he creates messes everywhere at your business.

One of the most interesting things about the Gorilla is you *think* you can't live without him.

His skills are nice to have around. You're used to having him around. But there's a ball of pain nagging at you when he make messes.

FRENEMIES

It's a fact. The Gorilla, like many great supervillains, is usually a close friend or family member who has been with you since the beginning of the business. Of course there are exceptions to the rule, but a good 75 percent of the time, the rule holds.

This makes the Gorilla a particularly difficult problem to solve.

All too often the Gorilla starts as a sidekick: an awesome sidekick who made a lot of sacrifices for you and your business . . . in the beginning. You depended on your Gorilla, and he was a big part of the business when you got started. He did a *lot* to help the business grow.

Yet, as the business grows, as it gets bigger and bigger, the Gorilla gains a sense of entitlement. He starts to think he can get away with bending the rules, ignoring systems, showing up later than everyone else, treating customers poorly, and spreading gossip around the workplace because you're so dependent on him.

Then the Gorilla starts to thump his chest like a drum.

Gorillas don't do these things on purpose, even though it feels like it sometimes. They don't just wake up one morning saying, "Wow! I can take advantage of the situation. I got this business owner in my hip pocket!"

The reality is the Gorilla's sense of entitlement comes from the natural evolution of the small business as it grows. The Gorilla feels like he's grown with the business into a position of privilege.

YOUR GORILLAS

One client of mine, who I shall call "Bubba," had such a Gorilla. His was an insanely talented brother who was willing to work for cheap. He would call clients, lug around heavy equipment, and drive Bubba halfway across the country without sleep. He did all this for his brother because, well, he's his brother. Bubba said he appreciated his brother's talents and hard work and skill and effort . . . *but* . . .

But what?

Like Pee-wee Herman said, "Everyone I know has a big 'but.'" If you have an employee with a "big but" at the end of his or her resume, you, my friend, have a Gorilla.

Gorillas exist at the extreme ends of the spectrum. On one hand, they're almost always good at what they do for you. Yet the "big but" reduces, if not negates, the value they bring to your business. For some Gorillas, it's explosive anger toward you, the owner, and even your clients. For others, it's the gossip they spread among employees. For some, it's the continual testing of your boundaries and rules by showing up late and misusing expense accounts.

You swear you won't let it happen again. You tell yourself that tomorrow it will get better. You try moving them to a different position in the business.

But it doesn't change. But it doesn't get better. But the same problems reappear.

But . . . but . . . but . . .

"YOU NEED ME!" the Gorilla thunders in the nightmares of your fitful sleep.

Sound familiar?

WHY THE HESITATION?

Likely the primary reason you let your Gorillas get away with this stuff is because they're so close to you. Friends and family are hard to deal with, especially in business, because owners let them get away with things they would fire other people on the spot for doing. Your brother or sister is a lot harder to fire than someone you hired right off of the street.

Some of my clients have even felt that customers were loyal to their Gorilla. They felt that if the Gorilla left, so would customers. However, after they let their Gorillas go, they were surprised to find out how many of those customers were, in fact, loyal to *the owner*.

Perhaps your hesitation is due to misguided kindness. One client of mine, even after identifying his Gorilla, let the misery drag on for almost *one year* in the name of being a "nice guy." He didn't have the heart to deal directly with the mess-making employee. When he finally had enough of his Gorilla's she-nanigans, he let that employee go. But by that point, tens of thousands of dollars and thousands of hours had been lost.

If that is your case, understand that the reality is, by letting an employee like this get away with Gorilla-esque behavior, you are actually HURTING them. It is incredibly unkind because you're keeping them from moving forward and growing as a person.

You might even be surprised when you finally work up the nerve to take care of your Gorilla. In my clients' experience, nine times out of ten the feeling is mutual. Why? One of the big reasons a Gorilla feels so entitled is because they sacrificed, sometimes a lot, for your business. So, the Gorilla becomes disgruntled and starts acting out, making messes and breaking things. Your Gorilla's sigh of relief after you fire him might just surprise you. They stick around because they think your business will implode if they leave.

Once you get rid of the Gorilla you will be surprised by how quickly other people fill the roles they left behind. Business owners often feel silly after they let their Gorillas go. And, occasionally, they're embarrassed when they realize they could have taken action a long time ago.

The Immediate Fix

There are two types of solutions to the Gorilla problem: one immediate, one long-term. Let's talk about the immediate fix first. Odds are you desperately need it, especially if you are close to your Gorilla.

To get immediate relief, there are only two things you can do with the Gorilla:

> # 1. PUT 'EM IN A CAGE
> # 2. RELEASE 'EM INTO THE WILD

CAGING A GORILLA means reinforcing existing systems or creating new ones to govern his behavior. This is one of the best ways to modify a Gorilla's behavior. You draw boundary lines he cannot cross; otherwise, you let him know he will be looking for a different job. Give him a clear set of standards and guidelines.

How does this work? You sit down with him and have a conversation about the behavior you expect from him going forward. Sometimes it's hard to sit down and have this conversation, but it is the first thing you have to do if you want to avoid releasing your Gorilla back into the wild.

RELEASING A GORILLA INTO THE WILD is exactly what it sounds like. You let him go so he can find an opportunity that better suits his traits and skills. If your company isn't a fit for him, there is likely a better fit out there . . . somewhere.

Most entrepreneurs prefer to start with the cage step, which is fine. Once you redefine systems for and convey new expectations to your Gorilla, it's time to step back and see how he reacts, whether or not he makes meaningful changes to his behavior. Sit back and watch.

Does he adopt the new systems? Does he convert back to being a helpful employee? Good! Then you may be able to rehabilitate the Gorilla.

But does he shake the cage? Rattle the bars? Does he make noise and try to kick it around? If he does these things, it's time to release him back into the wild.

Sometimes all a Gorilla needs is an opportunity to turn his attitude around and become a model employee again. If you build a good enough cage, using the right systems, and everything "clicks" in the Gorilla's head, this method can be tremendously successful.

Occasionally though, despite your very best efforts, it can also backfire. This is one of those situations where it's okay to be prepared to fail.

If you have an employee who is not happy working for you, and you are not happy with him working for you, you are practically doing that employee a favor by firing him. This dynamic between your Gorilla and your business isn't healthy for your Gorilla either. You owe it to your Gorillas to give them the "push" they need to find a place in the working world where they fit, where they can be truly happy. If it's not with you, then encourage them to find something else by releasing them from their obligations to your business.

One last comment for the more kindhearted among you. You know who you are. It's wonderful to be helpful to people. Just remember that you have *other* employees and families who are depending upon you. When you allow a Gorilla to shake the foundations of your business, you're letting him corrupt not only your own livelihood, but the livelihood of all your other employees and their families as well.

So, remember: releasing a Gorilla into the wild is still a success—for you, for that employee, for all your other employees, and for the business.

THE LONG-TERM FIX

Now let's get a Focus Tool into your hand that will protect your business from all future Gorillas. This is called the Most Valuable Employee.

Start by making a list of your top three favorite employees, the people you just can't get enough of at your business.[5] If you can't think of anyone working for you currently, then think of someone from your business's past. Write their names down here:

1. _____ Kendra _____
2. _____ Rachel _____
3. _____ Emmett _____

---

5.   A full worksheet in a nice one-page format is available for you at FocusedBusiness.com/mve. You're welcome!

Now let's take a good, hard look at the skills and traits that your favorite people possess. Traits and skills are often confused, and it is important for me to clarify the difference between the two.

TRAITS are personality characteristics of the employee. These are things they're born with, things that are genetic, things that your best employees have "built in" when they come to work for you. Traits are, in a practical business sense, *unchangeable*. They are an innate part of a person's personality.

"Loyalty" is a trait. Imagine trying to teach an adult about loyalty who doesn't already get it. They may know about "loyalty" in an intellectual sense because they can define it. However, getting a person to become "loyal" when they don't have it in them to begin with will be a struggle—one you probably don't want to pursue.

SKILLS are things people learn. Nobody was born knowing how to use Microsoft Office, or how to build websites, or how to sell using your particular method; however, these are all things that can be taught and thus learned.

"Good communication" is a skill. Training programs abound to help employees learn how to listen better and communicate with empathy. One may correctly argue that a trait such as "compassion for others" might help a person be able to learn how to better communicate. However, since almost anyone can improve in this area with some training, it would be considered a skill.

It's your turn. In the chart below, list the *traits* and *skills* for each of the top three employees you previously chose.

NAME	TRAITS	SKILLS
1. Kendra	- Honest/straight forward - Loyal - energetic	- communicat - people
2. Rachel	- Happy - Efficient - logical	- organized - communicat
3. Emmett	- logical - energetic	- organize - communicat

Now let's bring it together. You're going to take all of the stuff you wrote down about your favorites' traits and skills and create a profile of your Most Valuable Employee or MVE.

The MVE is not an actual person at your business; it's a profile of the ideal employee you would like to have working at your business.

Imagine if, instead of drafting the best player in a particular position, your favorite football team drafted the best available athletes and taught them how to play new positions. They would probably make it to, if not win, a couple of Super Bowls. In fact, Tex Schramm did just this with Tom Landry's Dallas Cowboys back in the '70s. The 1970s Dallas Cowboys were a force to be reckoned with because Schramm hired the best athletes and taught them to play the positions the team needed.

Traits are what make an athlete great. These traits make great athletes more capable of learning many skills, playing many positions. This is exactly what you're going to do with the MVE. You want to hire employees with the right traits, who are capable of learning the necessary skills if needed.

The alternative is what most small businesses do: they hire the people with the skills they need, only to have those people not fit in with the company's culture. These are people who are great at what they do, but it drives you nuts to work with them. In short, most small businesses hire and cultivate Gorillas. Messy. Costly.

Instead, create your MVE and hire to that profile. Hiring to the profile means hiring people who will thrive no matter what position they occupy. Then you'll rarely have to worry about employees driving you nuts.

So, last step. Looking at everything you wrote down previously—the top three employees, the traits—come up with a list of three traits that define your Most Valuable Employee's profile. Write your answer here:

OUR MOST VALUABLE EMPLOYEE HAS THESE 3 UNIVERSAL TRAITS:	- Loyal - Logical - Honest

"I NEED A WHOLE NEW COMPANY!"

Everyone knows what it's like to be rejected, and some of us hate it so much that it's hard for us to reject other people. Some of us are so heartfelt that it's hard to conclude that someone else is fundamentally incompatible with our businesses. So we string them along, painfully, for months, allowing their career to die a slow, miserable death.

Instead, what we want to do is quickly identify those who fit the company culture and let those who *don't* move to a better place. That better place is working for someone else. It will be better for the employee and better for your business.

So, once you have the three traits of your Most Valuable Employee, the next step is to write down the names of *everyone* who works for you.

Then put a "yes" next to your employees who possess *all* three traits. Put a "no" next to the names of your employees who are missing one or more traits. Put a "maybe" next to the people's names who may or may not be missing one trait, yet you would like to give the benefit of the doubt.

Now tally all the "yes," "no," and "maybe" answers.

What percentage of employees at your company don't have the traits your business needs? Over 50 percent? Seventy-five percent? One business owner, when I took him through this exercise, confessed candidly that he now realized he needed an entirely new company!

Ask yourself the cost. How much money is it costing you to keep these people who do not fit in at your business working at your business? Depending on their positions and your revenue, it could be millions of dollars. Ouch.

The idea is to fill your company with MVEs, people who are at the top of their game and match your company culture. Most companies are filled with LVEs, or Less Valuable Employees. When that happens, CHAOS Inc. begins to destroy your business from the *inside* out.

The trick is to eliminate your LVEs and ensure every position is filled by those who have the traits required by your Most Valuable Employee profile.

You Can't Copy Culture

A word of caution: every business has a different MVE profile. You can't just look at a successful company, copy the traits of their employees word-for-word, and expect to achieve the same success. You have to come up with what works for your business. Zappos has great employees—for Zappos. My company would never hire them, though. They are amazing employees and masters of customer service, but they're too crazy . . . seriously. They like to party too much for my business. I need some order. But the Zappos profile works for *Zappos*, and that's what counts.

Going through this exercise with business owners, I've found every business owner comes up with a different profile for their Most Valuable Employee. The good news is there's a home for everyone. Your Gorilla will find a nicer place to work after you release him back into the wild.

Protect Your House

Remember, the people you marked "no!" for lacking the traits your business needs are not happy working for you. They'll never get the opportunity to grow at your business because they just don't fit. They deserve to seize that opportunity with another business, a business that suits their traits better than yours does.

Of course, letting people go is painful. Just remember that you are doing them a favor. Help them with the transition if you feel you should. The point is to take action before they do further damage to your business.

As the superhero to your business, you can use the profile you created to ensure that all employees, from this point forward, are Most Valuable Employees. You can keep the Gorilla out—for good. I've seen firsthand many success stories of small businesses that have used this method to ensure the company grows stronger with every hire.

Cutting the Gorilla short will protect your business from most of the enemies that lurk within. Now we just need to address that enemy that lurks within *you* . . .

ACTION PLAN

Based on what you learned in this chapter, what is one action step you will take?

ACTION FOR CHAPTER 5:

list all empl. + check for
MVE Traits.

CHAPTER 6

YOU VS. MS. OPPORTUNITY

I magine you're attending a convention with a room full of entrepreneurs. I ask everyone to break off into groups of three or four. Each group goes to a table where I've set up a different assortment of random objects . . . popsicle sticks, Dixie cups, aluminum foil, and so on.

Your instructions are simple. Build the highest structure you can, using the object assortment at your chosen table. You can build it however you want because, hey, you're an entrepreneur, and you're going to do what you want anyway.

Can you see it? Each group building the highest structure they can, using random objects assembled on a table. Your group starts, and things are going well. Your building begins to grow.

But then, a couple of minutes in, the MC asks you to switch tables.

Can you imagine having to leave what you started, abruptly no less, only to have to pick up where someone else left off at the next table? On top of that, some other group is going to get your table and continue on where you left off.

But you dutifully proceed ahead, trying to figure out what in the world the other group was thinking when they made *their* mess. You begin building on top of it again, with mixed results.

And then, once again, the MC asks you to switch tables.

This process repeats for a half an hour, you starting to work on building something, then stopping, moving to a new table and starting all over. I've done this before with groups of business owners, and the result is always a very loud, very frantic disaster.

It's annoying when someone asks you to switch halfway through your project and start working on someone else's project. It's confusing to you. It's frustrating to your team. It's annoying. It's unproductive. It's chaotic.

So why then is it also the *reality* for most entrepreneurs I've encountered? Why do so many entrepreneurs jump on every last opportunity that comes their way, regardless of whether they've mastered the thing they set out to do in the first place?

Allow me to introduce another member of the staff at our evil sister corporation: Ms. Opportunity.

Ms. Opportunity

She's the Con's seductive sister and the VP of Business Development, Acquisitions, and Strategic Partnerships.

She's the one who tells you that you could make some fast cash doing something that has little to nothing to do with your core business. The Con gets you into business buried head down in the elusive dream of Ultimate Harvest. Then he tag teams his sister with a high five and hands you off.

Ms. Opportunity then distracts you from your core business. She's the one who shows you all those "bright shinies" and gets your heart racing with the thought of all the money you could make. Her motto is, "Never leave money on the table."

Ms. Opportunity persuades you to diversify too early. She cons you into expanding your line before you're ready. When you listen to Ms. Opportunity and take action based on what she says to you, just like in my example, you're switching tables and building something different on your own accord, without some annoying MC asking you to do it.

Even though in the back of your mind there's a little voice that tells you this is just going to create more chaos, entrepreneurs still switch gears, change businesses, and chase different opportunities all the time. We do this because the new opportunity looks exciting. It's sexy. It draws us in. It gets our hearts racing, thinking about piles of gold that would make Smaug envious.

But ultimately you're doing yourself a disservice by not sticking with your business's core.

BRIGHT AND SHINY

Opportunity is the entrepreneur's diamond. Opportunities, like diamonds, are bright and shiny, and entrepreneurs get excited when they recognize them. You're doing something and making money, and then you see someone else making money doing something else, right? You look at what they're doing, and you say, "Wow. That looks juicy. It's making my mouth water. I could make some money myself doing that . . ."

The problem is you don't understand how it's done, or how to start, or all the work that was required before that point, so you just jump in and start trying to do it your own way. It's not like your way is wrong and their way is right. It's way simpler than that.

The cost of switching tasks adds up over time. Switching from one opportunity to the other takes time, and the time adds up. The cost of switching your attention from one thing to the other is called *switching cost*, and it adds up just as fast as any other line-item cost if you don't keep an eye on it.

We've discussed how this affects you on a *micro*, personal-productivity scale when we explored Jack-of-All-Trades. Well, when you do this on a *macro* product, project, and strategic scale with your business, you accrue massive amounts of crippling switching cost.

The result is a bunch of half-completed projects. Nobody likes a half-completed project. How much fun is it to read half a book or watch half a movie? Nobody answers only half of the questions on their driving test. Only got half of that major surgery done? How'd that turn out?

Half of something is just as good as none of something.

1/2+1/2+1/2=0

Every entrepreneur has a story about going after something that didn't turn out quite right. I certainly do. For instance, it's easy see what a vendor is doing and think you can do it, too. Dance studios get into making their own costumes. Interior designers who get into architecture. Painters get into window washing. *Anyone* who owns a commercial building tries to get into hosting weddings and other events at their venues.

All of these things are great opportunities, but when attempted at the same time, they cancel each other out. Energy, creativity, and time that could be spent building your core business is segmented and diluted by steaming piles of switching cost. Compounded opportunities create a whole that is far less than the sum of its parts.

Another problem with pursuing work you're not known for doing is, instead of having the work come to you, you're out there chasing the work. Instead of growing your existing business, you're starting a new one from scratch. Why start over when you're already into something good?

It's a lot more productive to stick to what you're known for, especially when you're so well known for it that the work is coming to you. That only comes with mastery, and it's impossible to master something when you are constantly branching out and chasing new opportunities.

Opportunity is like a drug, and Ms. Opportunity is your dealer. This section should have been called "Opportunity Junkies Anonymous." This is the blessing and the curse of being an entrepreneur.

It's easy to get excited about something like branching out and doing something new. For example, one dance studio I coached was spending a lot of money on costume rental. They decided that they could potentially save thousands of dollars each year by making their own costumes.

It seemed like a wise business move; a stroke of genius. That is until after months of struggle the owner found herself repeatedly crying, banging on some seamstress's door in the middle of the night before every recital.

If the thought ever crosses your mind that you have to branch out to save money, squash that notion into dust before it ever manifests itself in your life again. Branching out into something new and different rarely, if ever, saves money, both in the short and the long run.

It always costs money to branch out into what is new and different, largely because you're starting a whole new business from scratch. While it's good to be frugal at home, be profitable with your business instead. It's never a good idea to waste thousands of dollars to save a couple hundred dollars. Not only is it a money-losing proposition, it also creates a lot of headaches for you and your business.

Let's say you're an ad agency, and one of your customers asks if you do websites. You say, "Of course!" And then you spend the next week putting a team together to build websites. Your focus up to that point was radio ads, and you were doing some great radio ads. Now you're building a bunch of crappy websites. You went from doing A grade broadcast advertising work to building a reputation for doing C work as a fly-by-night web design firm. By saying, "yes!" to web design, you're saying, "no!" to your core business.

Whenever you choose to pick up a new line or a new product, you're saying, "no!" to the other things that you're already doing.

Not only is changing course halfway through the journey unprofitable, it also frustrates your employees. This is a huge cost to your business. Entrepreneurs forget that they aren't like their employees. Entrepreneurs are more flexible and adaptable than your average person . . . that's the euphemistic way of putting it, at least.

In comparison, your employees find it confusing when you branch out into new things before the business is ready. They may begin to voice concerns. Listen to your employees. Thank them for the warning sign. They know what's going on, and you will too, as long as you have sense enough to listen to them.

VANQUISH MS. OPPORTUNITY WITH YOUR MOST VALUABLE LINE

What are you going to do about Ms. Opportunity? What Focus Tool can you pull from your utility belt to thwart her evil designs?

First, imagine for a moment a bicycle store owner. She also sells parts and labor to fix those bicycles. Over time, she begins renting bikes, thinking it's similar enough to what she already does that it's easy money. Then she sees a hot trend in kids customizing their bikes, so she buys inventory to meet the trend. You can see how subtly and quietly new lines of products and services can accumulate. What began as one line—selling bikes—became an unholy mutation of many lines, with no end in sight!

Both you and the owner of that bicycle shop have to decide which of all these offerings you're going to focus on. Once you and the shop owner master the sale of that one line, *then* you can expand. So, which of all these opportunities is the Most Valuable Line or MVL?

On the next page you'll find a worksheet to complete.[6] If you don't know these numbers, just provide rough estimates—what I call "entrepreneur math." Then you might create an action step for this chapter to begin tracking costs and revenue associated with each of your product lines.

---

6.   You can also get a full, clean worksheet for easy download and printing at FocusedBusiness.com/mvl.

TURN THE PAGE

$\longrightarrow$

LINE	TOTAL SALES / MONTH	TOTAL EXPENSES / MONTH	NET PROFIT /MONTH
Music Lessons	20,000	10,000	10,000
Km	21,000	8000	13,000
Dance	2500	1400	1100
B. Day Parties	300	150	150
Books / Inst	200	100	100
Hall Rentals	50	0	50
Inst Rentals.	50	0	50

You can also get a full, clean worksheet for easy download and printing at FocusedBusiness.com/mvl.

TOTAL HOURS OR UNITS/MONTH	NET PROFIT/ HOUR OR UNIT	VALUES ALIGN (Yes, No, Maybe)	ENJOYMENT (0-10)	RATE
200	50	yes	10	2
300	43	yes	10	1
50	22	yes	8	3
2	75	yes	10	4
20	5.	maybe	2	5
1	50	no	5	7
3	16	maybe	1	6

- Start by making a list of all of the products and services your business offers.

- Now estimate the total sales of each service or product line for each month.

- Next, list the expenses *per item* or *per hour*. Of course you have fixed expenses across all lines. We're going to ignore those. You also have variable expenses, expenses specific to each line.

  NOTE: If you are selling a product, such as the ubiquitous widget, then focus on per *unit* numbers. If you're selling a service, such as legal advice, then you'll want to focus on per *hour* numbers.

- Now calculate the net profit per unit or hour. Let's say it costs $7 to produce and sell a $10 product. That leaves you with $3 net income, or profit.

- In the next column, input the total hours or units you sell each month of that line.

We're now done with all that numbers stuff. Now let's consider some personal questions.

- Ask yourself, "Does this line align with our company's values?" Are you selling products that match your company's beliefs? Have you ever started selling a product or service that doesn't match the values of your business? I've seen it happen. Put "yes," "no," or "maybe" in this column for each line.

- Next, ask yourself if you simply *enjoy* selling that specific product or service. The business exists to give you life and enjoyment, and if you're selling something that makes you miserable, make note of it. If you hate it, and it drives you nuts to do it and sell it, then you may consider if it's time to stop selling it. Sounds strange, I know, but it happens.

- Finally, rank each line, starting with #1 as the most valuable, #2 the next, and so on. When ranking, consider all three factors: Net Profit/Unit, Values Align, and Enjoyment.

Your number one ranked item is your Most Valuable Line or MVL. Congratulations!

Now what?

Cutting Dead Weight

The MVL exposes Ms. Opportunity's lies. She wants to tell you opportunities are out there, waiting for you . . . somewhere. The MVL tells you where the true opportunity lies, and it's right in front of you.

Instead of chasing bright and shiny objects in distant lands, you will begin to see the diamonds in your own backyard. Knowing what makes you most of your money will motivate you to focus on that instead of chasing new opportunities everywhere you look. Focus on what you do best and master it. Then and only then should you move onto the next bright, shiny thing you want to master.

Wash, rinse, and repeat until you achieve world domination.

But what about the LVLs, those pesky, quasi-profitable Less Valuable Lines?

Simply put, start at the bottom ranked LVL and ask yourself, "What is the next step to removing it from our offerings?" Then take that step.

Now I understand entrepreneurs fall in love with their ideas. It's easy to fall in love with a new product, a new line, and focus on all of the potential it offers your business. Been there, done that. Love is important; for a moment though, look at the stark-naked numbers. Is the line you are in love with making you money or costing you money? If it's costing you money, consider how much more money you could be making by doing *something else* you love equally, if not more!

Speaking of emotions, fear weighs in heavily here. Entrepreneurs are fearful of losing their customers when they cut a line. You would be surprised to find that the opposite is usually the case. Cutting the stinker products out of your business will give you more time to focus on your winners, and the better you do what you do best, the more customers you will have asking you for it.

DUMPING MS. OPPORTUNITY

In the end, focusing on your Most Valuable Line will help you recover a lot of what's known as *opportunity cost*. Like the free-loading gold digger that she is, Ms. Opportunity would have you spend all that cost on her harebrained schemes.

Remember: opportunity costs time and money. In most cases, entrepreneurs are doing ten different things, and nine of them are so-so profitable, while one of them is responsible for 90 percent of your profit. Why do that to yourself and your business? Focusing on the other nine opportunities that bring in 10 percent of the profit does nothing but distract you from where most of the meat is, which is your Most Valuable Line.

This is the product or service that brings you most of your profit. This is what deserves your attention and effort.

So, the next time the temptation arises to expand into a new line, consider how much it will really cost you, and what could happen if you instead invest all that time and effort into your MVL. Odds are, you've already got the diamonds in your hand.

And, please, go tell Ms. Opportunity, "It's not you, it's me . . . But mostly you."

Let's move on.

ACTION PLAN

Based on what you learned in this chapter, what is one action step you will take?

ACTION FOR CHAPTER 6:

Look at #'s in MVL's

make sure they're correct.

CHAPTER 7

YOU VS. SIPHON

S iphon represents the customer service side of CHAOS Inc.

She symbolizes a very particular kind of customer who comes to your business. At first, Siphon looks like any other good customer, looking for value. Once you start working with her, she bleeds you dry. Her ideas about value are different than your ideas about value.

Siphons look like good customers, and they may very well be good customers . . . *for someone else's business.* They're just not a good fit for yours.

Siphon and Ms. Opportunity often work together. Siphon comes into your business and asks for something close to what you do. Her favorite phrase is, "Can't you make an exception?"

Then Ms. Opportunity follows through, telling you there's money to be made here, so you expand a little bit. You're chasing another "bright and shiny." Then you find out shortly that you wasted your time helping this kind of customer. You didn't make any money. Or maybe you did make some money, but it drained the energy right out of you and your employees.

Siphon-ish customers will wear you out because you had to expand and add a new product or service line to accommodate them. They will relentlessly ask you to make exceptions for them or add features as the job progresses. You have to do a lot more for these customers than for the vast majority of your other customers. You then add features, enhancements, and exceptions where none needed to be made. Siphon often uses "feature creep" to bog your business down.

Worst of all, you may end up *apologizing* for things your best customers find perfectly acceptable or even *love*.

SIPHON AS SALES REP

Siphon-customers sometimes sell themselves to you, as though you're the luckiest company on earth to have the privilege of working for them. Some of them are very convincing. You might even believe what they're saying. After you hear their pitch, you're thinking to yourself, "Wow! It's going to be awesome working with these people! I'm super excited to get started on all the new and different things they're going to have me do!"

In case you didn't notice, your employees are rolling their eyes.

That's what happens when Ms. Opportunity teaches Siphon how to sell. With their forces combined, they know how to cost your business a lot of money.

Sometimes Siphon puts on her salesman hat, hoping she doesn't have to pay you for services rendered. Instead of money, she promises you exposure. Whenever someone says, "You're going to get great exposure from this," what they're saying is, "I don't want to pay you." Siphon is the customer who asks you for half off in exchange for exposure and then pays you late. She's the customer who calls you ten times a day, asking the same questions over and over again. She's so high-maintenance that she drives you nuts.

ONE PERSON'S TRASH . . .

It's important to remember that your average Siphon isn't a bad person or even a bad customer. Siphon is simply *someone else's* customer.

It's important to remember this because you don't want to get mad at these customers. An important part of running a small business is the enthusiasm you bring to customer service. A big part of why you got into business was to help people.

Don't get angry when a bad fit walks through your doors and starts asking for a trip to the moon and back. Simply tell those people they're not a fit for you, and then refer them to someone who can help them.

The Focus Tool we'll use to make things clear for you is the Most Valuable Customer or MVC. Knowing your MVC can help you easily and quickly identify Siphons in your business.

To understand how this works, imagine your typical Walmart customer walking into Nordstrom and asking the salesperson in the store to help them dig through the racks, looking for something that's cheaper. Walmart's Most Valuable Customer is Nordstrom's Siphon.

Imagine someone who likes shopping for jewelry at Tiffany & Co. turning up at Walmart's jewelry counter. Tiffany & Co.'s Most Valuable Customer is Walmart's Siphon.

It goes both ways.

Or imagine you own a recording studio, and you start producing an album for someone. We'll call him Bob. Bob thinks you're best friends because you're producing his next album. He starts calling you three or four times a day just to bounce ideas off you. He starts sucking up all of your time. You feel like you can't charge him for that time on the phone.

Saying, "yes" to the Siphon is the same as saying, "no" to your best customers. The time it takes to complete jobs for Siphon means you may end up turning down MVCs who are willing to pay you what you're worth, who have no interest in paying you in "exposure." Again, opportunity cost is a killer.

How Your Employees Feel About Siphons

Not only do Siphons sap the energy out of you, the business owner, they also sap the energy straight out of your employees. Your team is comfortable working within the systems that you've created. Taking on Siphons turns that dynamic on its head.

When you throw them into a situation with a Siphon, with customers who are always asking them to make exceptions, you're contributing to the chaos in their lives. You're making their job unpredictable and treacherous. And remember, as an entrepreneur, you have a *much* higher tolerance for risk than your employees do.

There's a good chance you're dealing with a Siphon when none of your employees want to work on that customer's projects. Consider it just one more early warning sign that CHAOS Inc. has infiltrated your business.

Your Worst Nightmare

Referrals are awesome, aren't they? Yes, they are. Everyone loves when they've done such a good job that their customers rant and rave about how awesome they are. Of course you want referrals. They're the kind of advertising that money cannot buy.

You do not want referrals from a Siphon, and the only way to stop Siphon referrals is to make sure you refer *them* to businesses set up to take care of them. If you cater to them and do a great job but lose your shirt completing it, you do not want them to tell all of their friends about how you went above and beyond for them. Now you're dealing with a big group of Siphons. You want to yell, "No!! Stop!!!" because this is not what you bargained for in the beginning. You stand to lose a lot more shirts as you take on more and more of the Siphon's friends as customers.

When you say, "yes" to one Siphon, you're opening your doors to all of her friends. Doing this means you're turning down the opportunity to work with your Most Valuable Customers. It also means you're opening yourself up to Siphon cancer.

There's also a flip side to the Siphon referral. We live in a social media world. Thanks to the Internet, anyone, anywhere, anytime can get themselves a virtual soapbox, stand on top of it, and tell the world whatever they want about their experience working with you. Working with Siphons who ask you to temporarily change your systems for them multiplies your potential social-media liability. You're just begging for public complaints. It's hard to do a good job when you don't have the systems for it.

I'm not saying that you're never going to experience criticism if you focus on your Most Valuable Customers. What I am saying is when you accept Siphon-customers, you increase the likelihood of receiving criticism; you're accepting work you're not set up to complete. Siphon-complainers use social media to amplify your failures.

INSULTING YOUR RELIGION

To show you how we can defeat Siphon and keep her from ever returning to your business again, let me provide a fun illustration.

Do you belong to the church of "i"? Are you an iDisciple?

What I mean to say is do you own an iPhone, an iPad, an iPod, or an iMac? Do you use Apple products? Don't worry if you don't. In fact, if you're an Android/PC user, you might get a kick out of this.

Think of something you love about your iPhone.

Maybe you love it because it serves multiple purposes. It's a camera, a phone, and a GPS device. You can also access the Internet and check your e-mail with it. Got that feature in mind?

Guess what? My Android device does all of that, too. It's just as good as your iPhone.

But your iPhone syncs with your iPad says you. Guess what? My Android syncs with everything, too. And it does it without any fuss. Not only that, but I can jack my phone into my computer and transfer any kind of file I want to, quickly and easily, without using iTunes. My Android phone is occasionally *better* than your iPhone.

Ready to fight, yet?

If you're thinking to yourself, *yeah, sure Dave, but how often does it crash?* iPhones don't get sick, slow down, or crash, right? Absolute, 100 percent BS. I've worked with enough Apple users. I know what happens to your phones. They crash just as often as any Android device, maybe even more often. My Android is *way* better than your iPhone.

Mad at me, yet?

If you own an iPhone and you love it like Steve Jobs wanted you to, you're pretty close to throwing this book in the garbage right about now. I've raised your hackles, rustled your jimmies, and made you angry.

Now, cool your jets, because this was all just to prove a point, a point that has little to do with the phone you use.

While Android-based phones can do essentially everything iPhones can do, Android users aren't known for being raving-loyal fans of the brand like iPhone users are of Apple. A lot of people who use Android don't even realize it's a Google product. To them it's just another tool for them to use. Android users don't love their phones in the same way iPhone users do.

The point?

UNDERSTANDING IS MORE IMPORTANT THAN FEATURES.

Apple knows their Most Valuable Customers—intimately—and they use some of the most brilliant marketing minds on the planet to offer their products to the buying public. They know exactly what to say and do to turn their customers into ranting and raving, loyal fans of their product line. Not just the iPhone, but their *entire line*.

Understanding your MVCs and marketing directly to them is far, far more important than adding features to your line on the fly to retain customers who cost you more money than they're worth.

It doesn't matter that my Android does everything your iPhone does. I could talk about it until I'm blue in the face, and you will never convert to Android because you're 100 percent loyal to your iPhone.

LVC Repellent

Are you going to pick up fringe groups? Are less valuable customers going to come through your doors after you start marketing to your core? Of course! That's fine, no big deal. But once you have a good picture of your Most Valuable Customer, you'll be able to see the outliers, the fringes, the Siphons that much better. You'll be able to spot them as they're walking through your parking lot.

If you want to focus on your MVCs, then you also want to push away—flat out repel—the LVCs, or Less Valuable Customers.

I am definitely an LVC for Apple. Why?

I don't prefer Apple because I'm a geek, and geeks on the whole like to tinker with things. We like to change things. We like to play with things. We like to fiddle and tweak our technology toys to meet our needs. Geeks like to have as much control over the things they tinker with as possible.

Apple doesn't like that—at all. Google the term "iOS jailbreaking," and you'll see what I mean.

With Apple, *they* control what you do with their machines. Steve Jobs ruled Apple with an iron fist. That's part of the reason why the Apple experience is so integrated. There's "the Apple way or the highway" when you're using an Apple product. *And that is perfect for the Apple Most Valuable Customer!* Apple's target customers don't like to fiddle with, tweak, and hack their stuff. These customers just want their stuff to work, plain and simple.

No shame in that. It's just not for me.

Your average geek despises Apple products because Apple forces him to use their products on Apple's terms, not his. In short, geeks like me are Apple's LVC. They repel guys like me as strongly as they attract iDisciples.

THE LOCAL EXAMPLE

Curious who *does* get my business, by the way? They are a local company, and a perfect example of a Focused Business in action.

The company is called PC Laptops. The bland name gives them top billing in search engine results. However, the company is not bland in any way. They regularly give away geeky gifts like video games and Batman headphones via social media. Their founder, Dan "The Laptop Man" Young, awkwardly apes pop culture in his ads and then finishes by declaring, "We love you!" It's obnoxious, but it works.

PC Laptops has a motto that is truly unique: "To make you so darn happy with your computer that if your friends even think about going anywhere else you get mildly hostile." I fit that bill. They build custom computers with names like "Annihilator," "Katana," and "Epic." They build exactly what I want, with premium parts, and I pay premium dollar for it. I gleefully refer all people in my neck of the woods to them.

Understand: this is *exactly* the same principle that Apple is following . . . just with a different MVC. Both PC Laptops and Apple made that happen by first painting a crystal clear picture of their Most Valuable Customer.

Even though you have a small business, you don't have to play small. You can go toe-to-toe with the big guys and beat them using the same principles they use.

In this case, the principle is

ATTRACT YOUR MVC. REPEL YOUR LVC.

Build *everything* about the customer experience with the MVC in mind, making it a thrillingly passionate experience for them. At the same time, make your business absolutely abhorrent to your LVC. Then Siphon has nowhere to go but *somewhere else*.

It all begins with you getting crystal clear about who your MVC and LVC are.

GETTING TO KNOW THEM

Start by listing your top three, real life Most Valuable Customers. Who are these people? They are the individuals *most likely to buy your Most Valuable Line*, which we discussed in the last chapter.[7]

Think about real, human-being individuals. If you own a company that mostly sells B2B products, your Most Valuable Customers and your Least Valuable Customers will be the names of the decision makers at businesses who may purchase your product.

I encourage you to be as specific as possible when you're identifying these people, just as you did with your employees earlier.

---

7.   If you rushed through or didn't compete that exercise, well, back up, Speedy! Go do it now.

Think of the customers that make you say, "Man I wish I had a hundred of these. These people are a JOY to work with. They're all profit. They send us referrals! We love these customers!"

You might be tempted to write down demographic groups or your Most Valuable Lines. Don't do that. We want the names of real people, people who bring so much to your business as customers you wish you had more like them.

You will find out why in just a minute. Who are the three customers you want to clone stamp all over your sales floor . . . the customers who walk through your doors with bacon falling out of their pockets?

Write those names down here.[8]

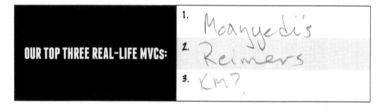

The next step is to compile their demographic information. What do these real customers have in common? List everything you can think of pertaining to their age, race, gender, income, and geography. This is all perfectly legal, and companies do it all the time. These are the criteria by which you will target future customers.

Most entrepreneurs know this customer info by heart. If you don't fall into that category, or you're so analytical that you want to conduct a six-month study to gather the data, *just give your best guess.* You accountant types can always come back to

---

8. This entire printable worksheet is available for free download at FocusedBusiness.com/mvc. Go get it!

this later and collate and quantify to your little heart's content. For now, though, just put something down.

DEMOGRAPHIC				
AGE	GENDER	INCOME	GEOGRAPHY	OTHER

Next, psychographics. Psychographics are what's going on in your Most Valuable Customers' heads. What activities do they enjoy? What are their interests? What do they believe in with all their hearts? What is their political persuasion? Who did they vote for last year? What are their attitudes? How do they feel about life in general? What are their values?

If you're not sure about this info, let me give you a secret: social media already has that information for you. Back in the day, the only way companies could get this kind of data was by paying a research firm tens of thousands of dollars to poll, survey, and census your customer to death. Now, by clicking on your biggest fans on Facebook, then clicking on the "Likes" section of their profile, you can get it. For free. Wow.

Take a moment and complete this psychographics section regarding your top three, real life customers:

PSYCHOGRAPHIC				
ACTIVITIES	INTERESTS	OPINIONS	ATTITUDES	VALUES

Now list your bottom three, real life Least Valuable Customers. These are the people who have been taking Siphon lessons in their spare time. List the three customers who give you and your staff the biggest headaches, the ones who cause you pain when you think about dealing with them. Which customers cause your staff to wince at the mere mention of their name?

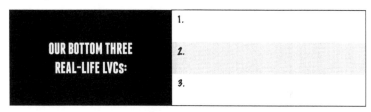

OUR BOTTOM THREE REAL-LIFE LVCs:	1.
	2.
	3.

Next you're going to compare the key demographic and psychographic differences between these two customer groups, the MVCs and the LVCs.

What are the most striking differences?

HOW OUR LVC DIFFERS FROM OUR MVC	
DEMOGRAPHICS	PSYCHOGRAPHICS

One final word: occasionally entrepreneurs find that their MVCs evolve with their businesses. I'd recommend you repeat the above exercise once every year or two, just to be sure you're still on target.

Now that you have this information you're ready to starting dividing and conquering.

Attracting Your MVC

Remember how I said you need to be as specific as possible when you're identifying your Most Valuable Customer? I never told you why, but I will now.

The best way, the most efficient way to focus on your MVC is to speak *directly* to them in your marketing. When you're marketing your business, you want to imagine you're having a private conversation with this individual. Cut all the corporate mission and vision crap. What do they *really* talk like and what do they *really* want to hear from you?

It's really very simple. The more you focus on your MVCs by speaking directly to them, the more business you will do with your MVCs. When you say, "yes" to that which is most valuable, you also say, "no" to that which is least valuable. We'll get into why this works in the next chapter about the Jumbler.

Did you surprise yourself and discover something strange, weird, or interesting that your Most Valuable Customers share? I'll give you an example.

I have a client who sells B2B stuff, and the decision makers his company works with all, without exception, live an active lifestyle. Their product has absolutely nothing to do with helping individuals be more active, but this is exactly the kind of people who convince their companies to spend the most money on my client's product. Something about them makes it more profitable selling to them than to couch potatoes. Jokingly this client suggested that maybe they should ask everyone who calls the office for their body mass index before going any further.

Kidding aside, you can actually use that kind information, the weird, unexpected information, to target your customers. In my client's case, knowing his MVCs tend to be active people who spend a lot of time outside, he could host a customer loyalty event at his business centered around an active lifestyle. He could sponsor a charity 5k to get his company's name in front of more active people He could call up his Most Valuable Customer and ask him if he wants to go on a hike or a walking meeting.

See how this works? The important thing is to use your knowledge of your customers to do things that identify with those customers and build loyalty with them.

It's a fact. Customers are more loyal to companies who align themselves with their interests. Look at Red Bull for an extraordinary example of this. They splash their name all over airplanes, racecars, and motorcycles, and they sell cans of carbonated, caffeinated, sugar water like they're five dollar bills on sale for a buck. Why? Because they've marketed to what their MVC loves.

THE DIVIDING LINE: PREQUALIFICATION

Once you know who your MVCs are, it's time to start prequalifying your potential clients by creating a system designed to zoom in on your MVCs. Let's say someone wants me to coach them. Even if they call me up and say, "I want you, Dave, to be my business coach," my response is never, "Great! Let's get started." That's just an open invitation for Siphon to set up camp.

Instead, I have *all leads* fill out the form to get a free action plan. I have them take the Chaos Assessment on my website and enter their e-mail to receive a free action plan.

In fact, please do that, right now. It will take about four minutes.

GO TO CHAOSQUIZ.COM

This exercise gives you a chance to see a prequalification system in action. But what happens behind the scenes?

The results of the Chaos Assessments then get forwarded to a live person on my staff. She uses the assessments to qualify prospects down one of three paths. I assure you this is not half as sexy as it sounds. The first is the "EMP" path, which stands for "employee," for a person who doesn't have a business. "NBO" is for New Business Owners, for your basic start-ups or solopreneurs. And "HGBO" is the path for High Growth Business Owners, established small businesses that match our MVC profile.

My assistant creates action plans that are specific to each type of customer. EMP and NBO are our LVCs. We refer them to other options to get my training, but that does not sap our company's focus. The HGBOs, though, get super special treatment. We have a certain process to follow up with them and give them the red-carpet, VIP treatment.

You too can use your knowledge about your MVC and LVC to create a prequalifying process. You don't have to use a website to qualify leads. Create a tool that fits your unique market. You can give physical surveys. You can ask questions when they walk into your office. You can have your sales team do a needs analysis before going too far down the road with a prospect. For larger sales you can do advance investigative research.

In the end, prequalification is simply about asking questions. Are you asking those questions, or are you jumping in for the sale, letting Siphon right through the front door?

Focused Businesses prequalify.

Repelling Your LVC

But what about the dregs of your customer soup? How do you get the LVCs to go away?

First, a comment about reality. For some entrepreneurs who suddenly realize that the majority of their customers are LVCs, there's a moment of panic. There's the fear, well placed, that the company may go bankrupt if you don't keep selling to these customers.

Tarzan swings from rope to rope to rope. Dropping your Least Valuable Customers is a lot like swinging to a rope that's not there. Before you can drop the draggers, depending on your business, you will have to scare up some winners. The only way to do that is to shift your strategy to repel your LVCs. Change how you work so that they will look elsewhere to get their Less Valuable needs filled, and I guarantee you that you'll naturally begin to attract your MVC. You can do that via price, message, or product.

Let's consider the example of one such massively polarizing company. Have you ever heard of Threadless.com?

They sell T-shirts with crowdsourced art, meaning that the shirts they print are created by users and then voted upon by their clients. It's an interesting model by itself. Yet the particular crowd they attract are geeks—like me. Which means the shirts people like have a very . . . unique . . . flavor.

I have a T-shirt from them, one of my favorite shirts. It's a picture of Alfred Hitchcock on a bench, surrounded by birds, but not just any birds: *Angry Birds*. Of the Rovio mobile game fame.

Another shirt is titled, "Zombie at Tiffany's." It features a zombified Audrey Hepburn striking her classic pose.

Get it? Pretty cool, huh? You'd wear it, wouldn't you?

No? You wouldn't wear it? Too silly, geeky, offensive, or inappropriate?

I promise I didn't bring this up to upset you. I brought it up to illustrate an important point about upsetting people. Upsetting people can be extremely valuable. Threadless doesn't want to be mean to people or to upset them; however, in the process of attracting their MVCs, they repel a lot of people who are disgusted by the stuff they sell.

If I hold up one of their shirts in an average room of business people, odds are only 10–15 percent of them would be comfortable wearing it. The other 85 percent or so people would be completely turned off by it.

Yet Threadless.com has a multimillion dollar business that a lot of people are struggling to replicate right now. Why are they struggling? Because it's damned hard to produce a product that is as polarizing as the products Threadless.com sells. It also takes unflinching fearlessness to produce and sell products that are guaranteed to cause controversy in the vast majority of the general population.

You don't have to be ridiculous or silly or disgusting to attract your MVCs. You just have to ask yourself, in your own way, "How can I target my MVCs better? And how can I send LVCs looking somewhere else?"

DESPICABLE ME (?)

Let's take family for instance. Family is a polarizing topic for entrepreneurs. Some entrepreneurs want nothing more than to spend all the time in the world with their family. Other entrepreneurs can't stand the thought of being in the same room with their family for any length of time.

The former are my MVCs. The latter are my LVCs. My guess is, the LVCs jumped ship right around chapter two when I talked about all that mushy spending-time-with-family-mini-harvest-stuff. Good. That allowed me to be much more candid, much more personal with *you*.

But I know there's a certain type of entrepreneur, mostly young guys right out of college. They believe that sleep deprivation is a badge of honor. Their goal is retirement by age twenty-six. These guys roll their eyes and run for the door whenever I start talking about how to spend more time with family. If I'm not talking about IPOs and venture capital and cashing in big or going down in a blaze of glory, I've lost them.

Do I try to cater to them to win them over? Heck no. I say, "Great. Head for the exits! Run faster, kids!" I'm not speaking to them. I'm not about to start speaking to them. They're not ready to listen. They haven't been down the road enough to the point where they're going to get anything out of what I have to say.

My message is about steady, consistent growth. It's about saving families, relationships, and *lives*. I'm now proud of that fact. But there was a time when I wanted to please everyone. I wasn't comfortable with the idea that some people wouldn't like me or what I had to say. I wanted to be *liked* . . . by everyone.

Then I grew up.

Remember: even though you have a small business, you don't have to play small. Most often, playing big means playing bold.

Be bold for your Most Valuable Customers. They're rooting for you.

ACTION PLAN

Based on what you learned in this chapter, what is one action step you will take?

ACTION FOR CHAPTER 7:

_____

_____

CHAPTER 8

YOU VS. THE JUMBLER

Are you starting to see how all of the information in this book builds on itself? We talked about your Most Valuable Line, the product or services worth the most money. We also identified your Most Valuable Customer. It's the person or business who buys your Most Valuable Line most often.

How do you get your MVCs to call you? How do you speak to them? How do you make them race to your shop in search of your product? How do you make them foam at the mouth for your product?

The way you speak to your MVC is with your . . .

Your what?

Your Most Valuable *Message*, of course. Before we

can get into that though, we have to talk about another baddie from the unlovely, loathsome people over at CHAOS Inc. His name is the Jumbler, CHAOS Inc.'s Chief Marketing Officer.

His favorite thing in the whole world is convincing you that your business can be all things to all people. He puts the bug in your ear, and you start saying things like, "We do it all! Anything! For anyone! We're the best at *everything!*"

YOUR CUSTOMERS ARE SOMEBODY, NOT ANYBODY

As the line from a Gilbert and Sullivan musical says, "When everybody's somebody then no one's anybody!" The problem with marketing yourself as someone who can do everything for anybody is your customers aren't just anybody. They're your customers, and they don't know what to think of you when you try to market your business to everybody. When you market yourself to everybody, your customers have no concept of what you do. This confusion hampers your customers' ability to make purchasing decisions.

To compound the problem, entrepreneurs often get hung up on which *method* to use to reach potential customers. The message is an afterthought, something tacked on at the end. They devote mounds of time and money fussing over whether to use the Internet, radio, TV, YouTube, mail, Facebook, postcards, flyers, or some new, crazy, harebrained scheme to deliver the message. All that time talking about TV and social media amongst yourselves, and you have no idea what you're going to say to your potential customers once you start trying to talk to them.

This plays right into the Jumbler's plans. He wants you to worry yourself sick over whether you should use the Internet or direct mail. He wants you to fuss over your website. He loves it when you spend all day learning about online advertising, thinking you're doing something productive for your business. All of these things make him feel all warm and fuzzy inside. He knows he's doing his job well.

The method you use is not even half as important as your message. Imagine spending a fortune buying media only to deliver a message that's off the mark. That's the worst kind of investment, the wasted kind. Yet entrepreneurs consistently repeat this mistake.

CONFESSING MY SINS

Entrepreneurs have a habit of falling in love with their ideas. We think a particular idea is so awesome, so incredible, so earth-shattering that we fall in love with it without realizing that it's only awesome in our own heads.

I've experienced this over and over and over again in my career. In fact, my biggest regret, my biggest mistake so far, was the title of my second book. *Invaluable: The Secret to Becoming Irreplaceable*. It's an asinine title. It's horrible.

How do I know it's horrible? I hire writers and designers to work with me, and every one of them since has asked me about it. They say things like, "Dave, if someone is truly irreplaceable, then there's nowhere for them to advance in their career. They're stuck. Because they can't be replaced. Why are you saying that?" Even my target market balked . . . unfortunately after the book went to market. They said, "As a business owner, why wouldn't I want to replace myself?"

As a result, it hasn't sold nearly as well as my first book, *The Myth of Multitasking*. Not even close. In my opinion, *Invaluable* is a far better book. *Invaluable* has some of my very best work in it. I practically turned myself inside out to write it.

Who cares?

The title got in the way of sales because people would look at it and think there's no way they want to be irreplaceable. The people who might have bought it had to ask themselves what the heck the word "invaluable" even meant. Does it mean the same thing as valuable or is it opposite or what? I muddled my message. The Jumbler jumbled my message. I thought it was brilliant until we printed it, and it went over like a herd of turtles in the marketplace. It sold okay, decent. But it didn't sell anywhere near as well as *The Myth of Multitasking*.

Why do we let the Jumbler do this to us?

YOUR EGO IS NOT YOUR AMIGO

Sometimes you're not ready to commit. Often you just want to be right all the time. You let Ms. Opportunity get the best of you. You're listening to Siphon too much. The Jumbler brings these both into play. He makes these concerns swirl around in your head and then vomit out of your mouth.

Sometimes it's just about fear. You're afraid if you say you *don't* do it all you'll lose customers and be unable to feed the hungry mouths back at home. A lack of focus often accompanies strong fear. The Jumbler exploits that.

Most often though, I think our egos get the best of us, like mine did when I decided to call my second book what I decided to call it. I'd rather not write the title out again. It's painful.

We want to look like we are capable of doing so much more. We want to avoid being pigeonholed into one area by our customers. Our egos—and the Jumbler—scream out from the inside, "We can do it ALL!"

There are writers out there who hate being called writers. There are a lot of artists who hate being called artists. Business coaches don't want to be lumped in with the *other* business coaches who have stained the industry. The painting company guy wants to be known for more. The school wants to be a one-stop shop. And on and on.

It all adds up to one thing: we don't *really* know what the heck we're doing. Admit it with me, entrepreneur.

Hold up your right hand and repeat after me:

"Even though I have moments of temporary genius, I admit that most of the time I don't know what the heck I'm doing."

Doesn't that feel better? The truth sets you free, right? Now that we've got that out of the way, we can get down to a real solution.

It turns out that the antidote to all this ego and confusion does *not* come from within, as a pop psychologist may want to tell you. At least in an entrepreneurial sense it doesn't.

The answer comes from the outside; in particular, your Most Valuable Customers.

Your Most Valuable Message Comes from Your Customers

Your MVC will help you define the Focus Tool you use to defeat the Jumbler. We call this tool your MVM or Most Valuable Message.

If you want to know what other people think of your business, don't ask yourself what you think of your business. What you think of your business doesn't matter. At all. We've established that your perception is distorted by both your ego and relentless confusion via the Jumbler.

It's what your *customers* think that is truly important. They will tell you how to sell to them if you ask the right questions. Open your ears and listen to what they have to say.

You can permanently wire the Jumbler's mouth shut by listening to your customers. It's that simple.

But not just any customers: your Most Valuable Customers. You identified them in the last chapter. If not, well, back up and complete that exercise before going forward!

MESSAGE, NOT METHOD

Unfortunately, even when entrepreneurs ask their customers about marketing, they're asking the wrong question. They ask a question about the *method* instead of the *message*, which is a huge mistake.

How many times have you seen this question on an Internet checkout form or doctor's office questionnaire or the like: "How did you hear about us?" This question is then followed by a list of eye-glazing options, such as "Internet," "radio," "word of mouth," and so on. Huh?

Absolutely, completely, utterly useless information. Most people have no idea where they heard about you. Even if they did, odds are you're too busy—you entrepreneur, you—to look at all the data and make strategic choices about how to use it anyway!

Okay, maybe I'm overstating the case. It's not complete crap. But it is premature. Spending on marketing is a big cost. If your message is wrong, you may spend a lot of money using the right method yet still get zero results. Or worse. When you're not clear about who you are and what you do, your marketing serves to attract Siphons and LVCs.

What we really want to know is *what it was* about your website, your ad, or what their friend told them that made them want to do business with you. You don't want to know *how*. You want to know *why*.

You don't have to pay a marketing company tens of thousands of dollars for surveys and focus groups to find out why your customers do business with you. All you have to do is ask them yourself.

WHY DO YOU DO BUSINESS WITH US?

First, please don't ask *everyone*. Don't ask your friends and family. Definitely don't ask your spouse. Don't even ask all your customers. Be focused. Otherwise you may get answers from Less Valuable Customers who buy your Least Valuable Line, which will put your business squarely on a trajectory toward chaos.

Instead, ask your Most Valuable Customers. Remember them, the ones who buy your Most Valuable Line? They are the key to learning your Most Valuable Message.

All you have to do is ask them, at the point of sale:

"Why did you choose to buy from us today?"

They'll be more than happy to tell you.

It might even be more useful to ask them questions like

"Why do you think we're cool?"

"Why do you like doing business with us?"

"What did you like about our website?"

"What did your friend say about us?"

Ask the right questions to make sure the answers you get matter.

Your Assignment, Should You Choose to Accept It

In order to build your Most Valuable Message, we need to gather some information. This is a critical activity, and one of the rare assignments you won't be able to complete while reading this book.

I recommend you ask the "why" question for at least two weeks, if not a month. Create a simple spreadsheet with four columns

- Customer Name
- What They Bought
- Are They MVC?
- Why They Bought

Then encourage your employees to ask a question like, "Why did you buy from us today?" Have them ask it right at the moment your customer gives you the money.

Why that moment? Because the answer will be fresh in your customers' minds, and it will be more accurate. If you ask a loyal customer after they've worked with you for a year, their answer will be biased. The Most Valuable Message is about what brings *new* customers into working with you, not necessarily what keeps them with you in the long run.

After you feel that you have enough responses, go through the list and

1. Eliminate any answers that didn't come from your Most Valuable Customers.

2. Circle commonly repeated phrases or concepts.

3. Write a one to three word summary of the repeated ideas.

For instance, if people often mention words like "friendly," "nice," "kind," "helpful," or "inviting" you might summarize them all with the phrase "friendly atmosphere." If they use words like "fast," "quick," "efficient," or "convenient" you might summarize them with "fast." No need to get creative or clever yet. That will come later.

The one to three words that summarize those ideas are now your MVM.

MY BUSINESS'S MVM IS

———————————————————————

What the MVM Is and Isn't

Sometimes when my clients first learn about the concept of Most Valuable Message, they try to equate it to other marketing-jargon-buzzword concepts they've heard in the past. Is it the same as a Unique Selling Proposition? Is this my company's slogan? Should I use this as our tagline?

The answer: absolutely not. The MVM is nothing more than the root reason why your Most Valuable Customer buys your Most Valuable Line. It is a simple foundation upon which we will build the rest of your marketing.

The problem is, most small businesses try to build things like a slogan and USP without the solid foundation of an MVM. They start with brainstorming creative ideas and phrases that look good on paper and might sound nice in a jingle. That gets us back to ego and the Jumbler.

Slow down there, Madison Avenue hotshot. You'll get a chance to show your stuff. First, just build the foundation. One to three words. Most Valuable Message. Keep it simple.

You're not trying to be an award-winning advertising agency. All you're trying to do is come up with the reasons, simple reasons, people do business with you instead of your competitors. You're trying to get to the core of why people want to do business with you. Throw all the junk in your head about being creative straight out the window.

Once you have your Most Valuable Message, you can hire a professional creative person to make your message sexy and magical for you. In the meantime, give yourself a break. Stop with the brain damage. Your MVM is not about creativity. It's about why they do business with you, plain and simple.

MESSAGE IN ACTION

Before we show you how to implement the Most Valuable Message in your day-to-day marketing and operations, let's consider a couple of examples.

I've asked raving Apple fans why they love their beloved i-everything so much. The MVM? Simplicity.

Apple sells the fact that their products are simple to use. That's what they use their marketing to teach their customers. Their marketing works because they never stray very far from their core message of, "Our products are so simple to use, you'll fall head over heels in love with them." Again, that's not a slogan, not a tagline, just a message that permeates every aspect of their marketing.

What about Disney?

There could be a couple of options, but if you look carefully at their messaging and marketing, I believe it to be: Magic. Every last bit of their marketing conveys ideas of magic: using stars and mythical beasts and Tinkerbell herself flying right out of their logo whenever one of their films starts playing. "Magic" is the first thing you see whenever you start watching a Disney film.

What's the first thing that comes to mind when someone says Walmart? Cheap. No hesitation, straight to the point. You go to Walmart to get your stuff cheaper than anywhere else.

Instead of "cheap," Walmart says, "Save money. Live better." That's the story they tell in their marketing, and they don't stray from it one bit.

Now it's your turn. List your favorite company . . . pick a different one than the three I just mentioned. Then take a look at their website, product, and packaging. What would be your best guess as to their Most Valuable Message?

COMPANY NAME: _____

WHY DO I BUY FROM THEM?

_____

_____

_____

WHAT DOES THEIR MOST VALUABLE MESSAGE SEEM TO BE? (1 TO 3 WORDS)

_____

Now that you can see how it works in other businesses, let's get to work on yours.

CREATING A MARKETING PALETTE

If you're an artist and you paint, you're going to need a palette of colors with which to paint your masterpiece. When you're marketing your business, you need a palette, too. That's what we're going to create right now.[9]

Your marketing palette is more than just color though. Your palette also consists of words and emotions and feelings. Your palette contains the tools you're going to use to paint the picture of why your customers do business with you.

---

9.   Yep. You can download this worksheet for free, too. Go to FocusedBusiness.com/mvm.

If you've ever written a story for a creative writing class, you probably remember your teacher telling you to, "Show! Don't tell." That's exactly how you want to approach your marketing. Don't tell your customers who you are. Show them instead.

If Apple is all about simplicity, what colors do you see most in their advertising? What does their palette look like? It's black and white. It doesn't get any simpler than that. Take a look at their first "Think Different" commercial, the one Steve Jobs narrated, from 1997. It consists of black and white video clips of some of the twentieth century's most influential people.

What if your Most Valuable Customers told you they do business with your auto shop because it's "clean." To get ideas, look to other companies or products that have "clean" as their MVM. What about Mr. Clean makes him the cleanest man alive? It's the sparkle, right? His shaved head, the smoothness of it. If we were to show our customers a pic of the shop in question, we would want to see some shine on everything in the pic, right? Of course. Everything should be spotless, shiny, and angular with clean, geometric lines.

Look at any company that has unified marketing, and you will see that they stick to a particular palette of words, colors, and images . . . even sounds, smells, and tastes where appropriate!

BRAINSTORMING

You called your best customer, the one you like dealing with the most, and you popped the question. You asked him why he does business with you, and he told you it's because you have the cleanest shop in town. You're organized. What does your palette look like?

What are you going to use to paint the picture you're going to show off in hopes of attracting more of your Most Valuable Customers?

I recognize that, for some, this exercise can be a challenge to start cold, so allow me to share an example. Let's say we've determined our customers have told us our MVM is "trust." My marketing palette might look a bit like this:

MARKETING PALETTE	
WORDS:	trustworthy, reliable, honest, loyal, dependable, believe in us, consistency
IMAGES:	home, grandparents, family, friendship, genuine smiles, seals of approval, real people
SOUNDS:	actual testimonials from real people, conservative music
SMELL/ TASTE:	baked cookies, leather, money
OTHER:	awards we've received, positive online reviews

Take a moment and complete the marketing palette form below. Don't try to get it perfect or 100 percent complete. Just jot down whatever comes to mind right now.

MARKETING PALETTE	
WORDS:	
IMAGES:	
SOUNDS:	
SMELL/ TASTE:	
OTHER:	

WRITING A KILLER, EYE-GRABBING HEADLINE THAT ATTRACTS YOUR MVCS

You have your first draft palette. Now it's time for the fun part. It's time to paint a picture. It's time to write a headline that describes your business. Writing a headline to describe your business is the first step to take to start attracting your Most Valuable Customers. It's also a lot of fun.

You may want to do it with a group. If you don't have employees, I've found that entrepreneur mastermind groups are a great place to give this a try.

Come up with headline ideas, based upon your Most Valuable Message as fast as you can. Creativity is more like a lightning bolt than a marathon. The more you churn and burn through your ideas, the more likely you are to land on one that works. Don't get married to your headline ideas. Don't fall in love with them. Ignore the inner critic—especially the Jumbler. Let yourself and your group run wild.

The key to doing this right is speed. Forced environments often lead to increased creativity. Creatives, especially writers, often wait until the last second to start working on your projects. Something about being pushed right up against a deadline makes the words flow for them. Pretend to be a writer who is up against a hard deadline.

I want you to come up with at least ten ideas in ten minutes. Get a timer out, and force yourself to write down absolutely anything and everything that comes to mind.

Ready? Set. Go!

1. _____

2. _____

3. _____

4. _____

5. _____

6. _____

7. _____

8. _____

9. _____

10. _____

Good work! Some of those headlines look really good of them . . . well, not so much. But how do we know w. ..er they *really* work? Which of these ideas will *really* generate sales, instead of just sounding cool or clever.

Two Words

We've got a solid foundation. Your headlines are based upon a marketing palette consistent with your Most Valuable Message. But up to this point, it's all been theoretical. Now we actually need to make money.

I have a lot of friends who are a whole lot smarter when it comes to marketing than I am. The ones I trust, the ones who really make a living with this stuff, live by a two-word creed:

Test it.

In other words, you don't really know which of these works until you run a campaign and compare the numbers. At the risk of oversimplifying it, it's really that simple. The only thing to keep in mind is that you'll never have it exactly right. You'll just constantly test and refine, seeing if you can improve results.

The easiest way to test ads, and perhaps the most cost effective, is to run a small-budget search ad test. Google Adwords and Facebook Ads are great places to do this. Create two different ads with everything the same except for the headline, bid on a couple of Google keywords and see what gets the best response in terms of clicks to your website.

Make sure to cap your spending though, because even though someone is clicking on your ads, this doesn't mean the page you're sending them to is going to convert them![10]

After you get your first results, tweak the headline or try a new one against the winner and test again. Once you find a winning headline, you can start testing changes in the copy underneath the headline, or the picture, or whether you capitalize this word or that word. But it all begins with the first headline.

You can do the same thing with postcards in the mail. Create an A postcard and a B postcard, mail them, and see which gets the best response. You can also take the same approach with some e-mail marketing programs. This is often referred to as "A/B" or "split testing."

If you've got enough traffic on your business website, you can even test internally. At the time of writing this book, if you visit the homepage of my website, **DAVECRENSHAW.COM**, you'll find at least four headlines on a rotating banner. They say things like

- *"Free Your Business From The Clutches Of Chaos!"*

- *"Harness Business Chaos, Harvest Personal Freedom."*

- *"Your Family Called. They Want To See More Of You Next Year."*

There were four headlines before we started using Google to test them. Based on the results of our testing, we dropped the fourth one and started focusing on these three instead.

---

10.   The landing page also needs to be tested and refined, which is a topic for an entirely different book.

The first and last word in marketing is testing. You must test your ideas to see what works, what gets the best response from your Most Valuable Customers.

Jumbled No More

In summary, get your own ego out of the way and let your best customers, your Most Valuable Customers, tell you why they buy from you. Then build a message, image, and brand around that. In this way, it will be organic, authentic, and irresistible.

Beating the Jumbler is surprisingly simple. He's had you thinking it's more complex than this. He wants you to invest lots of time, energy, money, blood, sweat, and tears into playing an endless guessing game. Don't believe it.

Your customers know the answer. All you need to do is ask them and then take action.

So, congratulations! If you've done all the work in the book up to this point, you've almost completely inoculated your business against CHAOS Inc. Only one more agent to go . . .

Action Plan

Based on what you learned in this chapter, what is one action step you will take?

Action for Chapter 8:

_____

_____

CHAPTER 9

YOU VS. OVERLOAD

L et's talk about the final agent at CHAOS Inc. Meet the Chief Information Officer, Overload. She's giving you so much information and so many different options it causes you to not know what to do or how to do it or worse—she makes you not want to do anything at all.

Overload is the charming young girl in the boardroom, hiding behind big glasses, who everyone underestimates. More information is good, right? Knowledge is power, yeah! In reality, she's using all that knowledge and information to pin you hopelessly under the thumb of Chaos.

She does it by constantly telling you one seemingly simple, yet ultimately damning, lie: "There's only one right answer."

As long as you believe that one best, right answer exists when it comes to your business, you

will keep searching, searching, searching until you find it. You have to! Maybe you should read another book, or attend another seminar, or talk to so-and-so, or do more Internet research or . . . on and on and on.

Overload's got you under her spell, making you think information alone is enough to solve your problems.

ANALYSIS PARALYSIS AND THE INCHWORM

Information overload has become a nearly unstoppable force in our personal lives. We have become addicted to a steady stream of glowing, electronic, luscious data. If we can't get it from a TV, we get it from a computer screen. If we can't get it from a tablet, we get it from our phones. Ah, the glorious, glowing screen. Stick a needle in, baby, and download a gigabyte!

But what happens when you give yourself too much data to analyze? You know those financial reports that do nothing but mystify and overwhelm you? Ever stared into the computer at one of those things and had your mind go completely blank for ten minutes at a time? Overload is responsible for that.

She makes you paralyzed, unable to do anything. This is Overload's secret weapon: the Analysis Paralysis Stun Gun, which shoots high-voltage information out of its barrel in heart-stopping quantities, enough to glue you to the back of your chair and keep you from moving your business forward.

It's the same thing that happens when you tell an inchworm he's going to have to crawl the next one hundred miles all by himself. He gives up the second he realizes how far he has to go, regardless of the fact that he was going to do it anyway. It takes a brave inchworm to keep crawling once he knows how far he has to crawl.

As a business owner, you can't afford to be the cowardly inchworm who, knowing how far he has to go, refuses to take the next step.

It's time to learn how to be a brave inchworm.

GET YOUR ?#@*% TOGETHER

Before we proceed, I do have to say that financial numbers aren't evil. They are necessary, valuable, and potentially very powerful . . . taken in small doses.

All too many small businesses have decided to deal with the problem of Information Overload by burying their heads in the sand and pretending financial reports don't exist. Don't ask me how they intend to pay taxes that way, yet they do it all the same.

Hire an accountant if that's what you have to do. If your numbers are a mess, then you probably don't have the skills or the time to dig yourself out. This isn't something you want to do yourself, no matter how good you think you are at math. Remember your Most Valuable Positions? Unless one of them is accountant, you want to hire an actual accountant to help you.

Seriously. Do it *now*.

Growing a business is like raising a child. Everyone's business is in a different place, a different maturity level, when it comes to gathering and analyzing data. Some businesses, especially new ones, don't keep track of their numbers. It's time to start keeping track of everything. Some businesses start gathering data before they open their doors. Everyone is at a different stage.

Don't be afraid of starting from scratch, even if your business is up and running. I don't want you to get the idea that information is bad. It's not bad by itself. It's bad when you don't have it and only gets worse if you don't know how to use what you have.

All that said, there's a massive difference between gathering the numbers and actually *using* the numbers strategically. Overload would have you think otherwise.

SIMPLIFYING YOUR FINANCIAL REPORTS

The key to using financial reports strategically is focusing on what's most important, the indicators that give you the most bang for your buck, so to speak. You are about to learn how to identify the numbers that matter most to your business. These are called your Most Valuable Indicators or MVIs.

Focus is the strategic allocation of your resources toward that which is of most value. In order to bring focus to your information overload, you have to know what information is of the most value, the most utility to your business. Overload rules the day when you have no idea what you're looking at or how to go about using it.

You've always suspected it, but I'm going to confirm a fact for you. Ninety-nine percent of the data you gather in your reports is absolutely useless to you as a business owner. As the owner of a business, you have to know what 1 percent of the data is important to you.

You only have to pay attention to *five* numbers. The rest have some value, but you can give the rest to your managers, employees, and accountant to worry about.

CASH ON HAND: MVI #1

Some people call this "liquidity," or liquid money. It's money you can access quickly and spend easily.

Cash is the lifeblood of your business. Cash creates opportunity. Cash creates security. Cash is *king*. The more cash you have on hand, the longer your business can operate without revenue. So your business needs a cash reserve, and it's called Cash on Hand.

You also need a steady influx of cash from customers to keep your business running. Cash is to a business what blood is to a living creature. If you start bleeding, it has to stop at some point or else you're going to star in your own funeral sooner rather than later.

But how much cash should your business have? There are two options.

The first option is the **THREE MONTH RESERVE**. This number is based on how much cash your business would need to stay open for three months without revenue. To put it another way, how much money would you need to not go bankrupt if you turned all of your customers away for the next three months?

If you have a line of credit, that will take a bit of pressure off of you. Your three month reserve can then be your current cash on hand minus your line of credit.

So, if you business would need $300,000 for three months, and your line of credit is $100,000, the number to target for cash on hand would be $200,000.

That's how you answer the question using fuzzy, funktified entrepreneur math. It's not the best way, but it will get you started.

By the way, it's a wise idea to secure a line of credit even if you are making a lot of money and have plenty of cash on hand. Banks don't like loaning money to broke people and broke businesses, even though that's when you will need the money most. The best time to ask the bank for a line of credit is when you *don't* need it. In other words, when you have lots of cash on hand. For the purposes of running your business, your credit line is just like money in the bank. It's your emergency supply.

The second option is **ASK YOUR ACCOUNTANT**. I know that sounds like a cop-out, but it isn't. They'll have the best perspective on how much money your business really should have to always stay liquid. Even if you came up with a three month reserve number, just to be safe, ask your accountant how much cash you need to keep on hand.

Then don't just take their word for it, go ahead and add another 30 percent to your accountant's number. If they tells you to keep $100,000 in the bank, aim for $130,000 in the bank, just to be safe.

It feels good knowing you have enough money in the bank to keep operating no matter what happens to your revenue. It gives you a platform of confidence to stand on when you're operating your business. Confidence is key when it comes to decision making. When you don't have enough cash on hand, you have little choice but to operate in a state of fear. This is exactly what CHAOS Inc. wants for you.

Fear is like a drone strike straight to the focus you're trying to achieve in your business. You're forcing yourself to operate in a state of chaos whenever you don't have your resources where you need them, and it all starts with keeping enough cash on hand.

One last word on this MVI: never let your cash on hand fall below your critical level. If it will help you stay disciplined, create a separate account at the bank to squirrel away your safety reserve. Then remember MC Hammer every time you're tempted to touch it.

Before you proceed, write your current cash on hand number here:

MVI #1: CASH ON HAND =

NET PROFIT: MVI #2

Net Profit is the second most valuable indicator you need to pay attention to at your business.

It's easy to get this number. It's the "bottom line." All you have to do is subtract your expenses from your revenue. This is the primary reason behind having easy access to financial documents like profit and loss statements. These documents make it easy to see exactly how much money your business is making for you.

It doesn't matter one bit how much you grow your revenue if you're losing money at the same time. This is important to keep in mind because there are many prestigious awards out there that are based purely on sales growth. I'm talking about the Inc. 500/5000, Fortune's Fastest Growing Companies, New York's Fast 50, and the like. Not that these awards don't have value; they just have the tendency to get entrepreneurs focused on a Less Valuable Indicator.

Business owners love making it on these lists, and some of them go whole-hog crazy, spending enormous amounts of money to grow their sales in order to make the list. But should that really be your primary goal? Awards like these don't take *profit* into account when they're making their lists. This is a massive shortcoming. It's a bit like awarding a tournament championship to the team who scored the most points . . . regardless of how many times they lost.

From a marketing perspective, being on these lists is great. It's exciting. Getting your business featured in magazines is a great way to get exposure. However, it's easy to kill your business chasing sales. To *Inc.* magazine's credit, they did print an article on some of the companies who made the list who *didn't* do so well in the following years. It's all too easy to do. All it takes is spending your cash on hand to grow your sales without paying attention to the expenses. Your business dies the second you run out of money.

You always want your revenue to beat your expenses. In other words, keep your eye on your profit, and you won't go broke tilting at windmills, chasing unicorns over waterfalls.

Before you proceed, write last period's net profit here. Use a time period of year, quarter, or month . . . however you think about it most often.

MVI #2: NET PROFIT FOR PRIOR PERIOD =

THE BEST HOT DOG CART EVER

Pardon me while I pause from the thrilling MVI list for a moment, but I need to share a profound small business example with you. There's no better place in the book to do it.

I once offered the owner of the best hot dog cart in the world some free publicity a couple of years ago. I wanted to interview him and tell his story on my website.

He turned me down.

He then told me he's turned down people who are a lot more famous than I am, starting with Martha Stewart. This got my wheels turning. Why would a business owner turn down free publicity from someone as high-profile as Martha Stewart?

Not only did he turn me down, he took the time to tell me why he was turning me down. Like I said, this is the best darn hot dog cart in the world we're talking about. Of course the owner is a good guy who is nice enough to explain himself.

He doesn't want any publicity because he doesn't want to mess up what he already has, and he already has everything he wants. He makes a solid high six figures a year selling hot dogs on the beach. That's enough to share his lemonade freely with anyone who approaches his cart. It's more than enough money for him to live the life he wants to live. He gets to work on the beach while he sells hot dogs, and he has lots of opportunities to talk to interesting and not-so-interesting people.

Let's say he tried to franchise his winning hot dog cart formula all over the country. He might be successful. He might not be successful. He's not willing to risk it because he already has everything he wants out of life.

He's a very smart man.

Chasing sales is sexy. Expansion is sexy. World domination is sexy. They're just not always the best ideas in the world. To the contrary, chasing those seductive sales numbers or the seduction of world domination is one of the best ways in the world to have a whole lot of fun and burn your business to the ground all at the same time. CHAOS Inc. rejoices while you and yours weep.

Of course, the people reading this book, at least the ones who made it this far, aren't the sort to spend every waking hour and every last dollar of borrowed money growing their sales. Running a business isn't as much about the big numbers for you as it is about getting what you want out of your life. I think that's a smart way to go about running your business.

Be the hot dog cart. Don't be the next wannabe pump-and-dump, fly-by-night IPO.

You don't have to go suicide-Rambo-mode on your business as long as it's profitable. Sales don't matter as long as you're profiting enough from your business to live the kind of life you want to live.

I'll now get off my hot dog cart soapbox. Let's continue.

YOUR SALARY: MVI #3

Salary? What salary?

If those are your first thoughts, you're not alone. This is one of the biggest mistakes I see entrepreneurs making, over and over again. They don't pay themselves a consistent salary. They don't treat themselves like the Most Valuable Employee at their business. Make no mistake about it. Even though made a profile of the MVE, the kind of employee you want to hire, you and I both know who is the true most valuable employee.

You are. And as such, you deserve to pay yourself a salary. Consistently.

When you pay yourself a consistent salary it provides a much needed foundation of stability, both in your life and the life of your family. It also creates a much needed foundation of stability for your business. A consistent payout schedule to you as the owner will protect the business's cash on hand.

For brevity's sake, when I say salary understand that I'm also including any dividends you may receive as a shareholder and owner. Your accountant can advise you as to what the best ratio of wages to dividends is. Just make sure that the payment to you is *consistent* and *predictable*.

WHERE TO BEGIN

In new start-ups, or occasionally in severely rough patches, you may find that your business just can't pay you a reasonable wage. I've been there myself.

In those situations, begin with *something*. Even if you set up a monthly salary of one hundred dollars, that's better than nothing. It creates a benchmark to grow from.

Like any other employee, from time to time you will want to take a hard look at your performance and decide whether or not you should get a raise. If I'm coaching you, from time to time I will pretend to be your Virtual Board of Directors, and we'll have a conversation about whether or not you deserve a raise.

Does that sound funny? If you're not paying yourself a salary, giving yourself a raise sounds awfully funny. Not only does it sound strange, you might even feel guilty about giving yourself a raise, especially if you're not paying yourself a consistent salary. What will your employees think? Who cares what they think of your salary? It's your salary, and you deserve to get paid just like any other employee at your business.

You're overstating your profit and your cash on hand if you're not paying yourself a salary. How profitable is your business if you can't afford to pay yourself a salary? You know the answer. If you're not paying yourself, then why in the world are you in business? There's only one answer, and that is because you got duped by the Con and his Ultimate Harvest lie. Overload just aids and abets the lie by keeping you so overwhelmed by the numbers that you don't stop to think about what you're *actually* making.

I'm not saying there won't be months where the crap goes through the fan, and you will have to sacrifice your own salary to make payroll. You understand that things are going to happen, and that's just the life of an entrepreneur . . . occasionally.

What I don't want you to do is make the mistake of saying, "I don't ever get a paycheck because I'm the owner of the business." I've seen so-called experts recommending entrepreneurs taking "whatever is left" out of the business, month after month. That's a mistake. You should get paid according to the value that you're bringing to the business. The rest can then be added to your business's cash reserves to be reinvested back into the business.

How Much Should You Pay Yourself?

Honestly, you should be one of your company's top paid employees. Depending on your company, there might be a rockstar salesperson or two who makes more money than you do, based on commissions, but you're the CEO, and you should get paid like you're the CEO of an equivalent-sized company.

Think about this when you're looking to cut yourself a paycheck. How much would it cost to hire someone to do everything you do at your company? Let's start at the bottom. Let's say you're not paying yourself a salary at all, but you're working at least seventy hours a week at your business.

Could you hire someone to replace you for what you're paying yourself?

Not legally because you're not paying yourself. Nobody works for free except for deranged business owners with screwed up business brains. If you're not paying yourself a salary, you're not even a legal employee of your own business because you're not even making minimum wage. You're a CEO who doesn't make minimum wage. Don't worry. You're not alone. There are lots of people out there reading this book and thinking the exact same thing.

You have to start paying yourself a salary, but how much is enough? How do you figure out an appropriate amount of money to pay yourself?

Many business owners get by with asking themselves, "How much do I need?" If you can be honest about answering that question, you'll answer it just fine. Once you're comfortable, and you don't have to worry about money, it doesn't matter to what extent you overpay yourself as long as your needs are met.

Also consider what it costs to provide for your mini-harvests. Thinking about these things can involve some mental gymnastics centered around what you know about yourself as a person. The answers to these questions are highly personal, and I would encourage you to think long and hard about them.

Maybe you're someone who doesn't need all that much. Some people have enough self-knowledge to know that they're perfectly happy where they're at, and things just can't get much better than that, like the owner of the best hot dog cart in the world.

For some people though, their numbers will never be big enough. This is the opposite of the hot dog cart story. It's the story about wanting to watch your business grow and grow and grow, and you won't stop until you've monopolized an entire industry. It's the story about the guy I used to coach who was literally making a million bucks a year, but he couldn't get over his buddies who were making three million bucks a year. He looked at himself in the mirror and asked, "Why can't I make three million bucks a year like my buddies do?" There is absolutely no end to that line of thinking unless you put a stop to it yourself.

In the end, just think of yourself just like any other employee at your business. Take care of yourself and your family, so you don't have to worry. Then as long as your financial needs are met, you can focus on your wants, and those tend to be way more personal than money.

Before you proceed, write the monthly salary you are either currently paying yourself or will begin paying yourself.

MVI #3: MY MONTHLY SALARY =

WILD-CARD INDICATORS: MVI #4 AND #5

The last two indicators are completely up to you, based on your business. These are the two numbers you decide are the most valuable, and every business has their own criteria. The way you start figuring this out is by asking yourself questions like, "What number relates directly to sales of my Most Valuable Line?"

Need some ideas to stir your thinking? Consider these options:

- Sales of your MVL

- Expenses associated with your MVL

- Number of complaints as an indicator of how well your employees are doing

- Expenses associated with acquiring your Most Valuable Customers. How many sales calls do you have to make to get one customer?

- Number of prequalified customers received in a period of time

- Number of sales presentations given

- Sales closure rate

- website traffic on a sales page

- Employee turnover

- Net profit on a project-by-project basis

All businesses are different. You have to decide for yourself what your last two MVIs are.

The temptation when you start thinking about your wild-card indicators is to want to track three, four, five, or more indicators. Don't fall for Overload's nonsense! If you're going to run a focused business, you have to learn how to allocate your resources toward that which is of most value. Some indicators are more valuable than others. The key to this is testing indicators that you think will be valuable, focusing on two of them at a time.

Track these for about six months, then if you don't find them valuable, you can always switch later. Remember: there's no one right answer!

With Overload neutralized, you have now assembled the tools necessary to defeat every agent of CHAOS Inc. Now it's time to put them all together in one convenient place.

Action Plan

Based on what you learned in this chapter, what is one action step you will take?

Action for Chapter 9:

_____

_____

CHAPTER 10

THE FOCUSED BUSINESS MAP

t's time to use what you learned in this book and put it into action.

The most important aspect of this book has nothing to do with words, worksheets, action plans, or exercises. The most important part of this book is when you take the things you've learned to your business and act on them.

At the end of every chapter I asked you write down just one action . . . one thing that you can do to improve your business and perhaps your life. If you followed this suggestion, you now have nine concrete things you can do to immediately triumph over chaos. It's a nine-step action plan.

If you have more than nine action points on your plan, I suggest you reduce the list. Doing nine things and hitting nine targets is plenty for you to focus on. There's no reason to add to the chaos in your business by trying to do too many things at the same time.

I suggest you do two things with this nine-step plan:

1. Open up your calendar and schedule time to complete just the next step toward completing each action in the plan. You may be scheduling items a year into the future. That's okay.

2. Tell everyone who will listen about the nine steps you'll be taking. The more you say something out loud, the more you share it with other people, the stronger your conviction to stay focused will become. Your public commitment will improve your private responsibility.

This nine step plan will be a powerful propellant toward your business goals. But there's still one more tool I need to give you before we wrap this up.

SEVEN AGENTS, SEVEN TOOLS

We're about to assemble everything you created in the previous chapters into one powerful tool.

First of all, let's review the Agents of Chaos and the Focus Tools *you* created to put them in their place, permanently.

THE CON		**HARVEST STRATEGY**
JACK-OF-ALL-TRADES		**MOST VALUABLE POSITION (MVP)**
THE GORILLA		**MOST VALUABLE EMPLOYEE (MVE)**
MS. OPPORTUNITY		**MOST VALUABLE LINE (MVL)**
SIPHON		**MOST VALUABLE CUSTOMER (MVC)**
THE JUMBLER		**MOST VALUABLE MESSAGE (MVM)**
OVERLOAD		**MOST VALUABLE INDICATIORS (MVI)**

Each of these tools is powerful on its own, but when combined, they form an impenetrable forcefield to help you build a Focused Business. I call this tool the Focused Business Map.

YOUR FORCEFIELD

The Focused Business Map is deceptively simple. On the next page you'll see one that you can fill out. However, I also recommend that you go to FocusedBusiness.com/map and download a clean version, which you can print out full-size as many times as you like.

MVIs
1. Cash on Hand (Current)
2. Net Profit (Previous Month)
3. My Salary (Previous Month)
4.
5.

MVE

MVL

MVC

MVM

MVPs
1.
2.

HARVEST STRATEGY		
	DAILY	WEEKLY
PERSONAL		
FAMILY		

This worksheet is also downloadable at FocusedBusiness.com/map

	QUARTER	
	LAST Q / PERIOD	TARGET / PERIOD
		START %
		START %
		START %
		START %
		START %

MONTHLY	YEARLY	ULTIMATE

Begin by copying the Focus Tool responses you created in previous chapters into their corresponding places in the Focused Business Map. Flip back through the chapters, find the answers you put, and write them down into the Focused Business Map. This will also be a helpful, quick review of the principles you learned in this book. Ignore the right hand columns for now; I'll talk about them in a moment.

Please go ahead and transfer your answers now. I'll still be here when you get back.

Done? Great!

Now, in five easy steps, you can make the Focused Business Map one of the most powerful tools in your entrepreneurial arsenal.

1. Post a copy of your completed Focused Business Map in a place where you can see it every day. I recommend framing the Focused Business Map and putting it on your desk or scanning it and making it your computer wallpaper.

2. Any time you are confronted by one of the seven Agents of Chaos, refer to the Focused Business Map. Remind yourself of your commitment to strategically focus your resources on only those things that are of most value.

3. Once per quarter, do a full audit of every item on the Focused Business Map. In particular:

   A. Measure your performance in the five Most Valuable Indicators. Write down how you did last period (such as quarter or month) and what your target is for the next time period.

B. Roughly assess how well, percentage-wise, your company is doing in moving toward a 100 percent ratio in the areas of MVEs, MVL, MVCs, and your MVM. In other words, if you think that 75 percent of your employees fit the MVE profile, then write 75 percent. If you feel that your message is mostly focused, but could use some work, put 80 percent in that column.

3. At the end of that quarterly meeting, create a new Focused Business Map, making minor adjustments as needed.

4. Return to step one.

It's that simple.

MORE THAN A PLAN

Examples are usually the best way to illustrate this process in action. On the next page, look at the example I've completed for you. This Focused Business Map is what yours might look like at the end of a quarterly review:

MVIs	QUARTER LAST Q / PERIOD	TARGET / PERIOD
1. Cash on Hand (Current)	$50,000	$60,000
2. Net Profit (Previous Month)	$10,000	$12,000
3. My Salary (Previous Month)	$10,000	
4. New Customer Inquiries	27	35
5. Sales Closure Rate	52%	70%

MVE	START %
Humble, Fun-loving, Persistent	80%

MVL	START %
Annual Maintenance. Packages	55%

MVC	START %
"The Jones Family"; Middle-Upper Income Families, Live in Suburbs, 1-2 children, single-income, conservative, "soccer moms"	30%

MVM	START %
Dependability	90%

MVPs	START %
1. Founder / Visionary	10%
2. CEO	15%

HARVEST STRATEGY					
	DAILY	WEEKLY	MONTHLY	YEARLY	ULTIMATE
PERSONAL	Exercise for 30 minutes while watching TV	Take half-day Fridays off	Day at the spa	Give myself a holiday bonus	Able to donate my time freely to charity and not have to worry about paying the bills
FAMILY	Focus on my family 100% from 6 pm to 9 pm	Date with spouse	Three-day weekend trip	Two week, "fully unplugged" vacation out of state	Dream Home; Freedom to tour the world with my spouse

Most of this example is fairly straightforward if you've read the book and completed all the exercises. The only thing new here is the percentage measurement, which is just the subjective number that you choose to represent how well you're doing. Your goal should be to get each of your Focus Tools as close to 100 percent as is reasonable.

When you set new targets each quarter, try to keep them as gradual improvements, rather than quantum leaps. This will keep you grounded in reality and more motivated to see your business improve.

This map is designed to be highly simple and yet very effective. You can almost think of it as a one-page business plan . . . except it has a lot less words, was a lot less painful to create, and you'll actually use it daily for strategic decision. Other than that, they're exactly the same.

Triumph, At Last

Focus first. Mastery second. Then diversification . . . if you still want it. This is the Focused Business Model. The Focused Business Map can keep you aligned with that model even when CHAOS Inc. does its darndest to destroy you.

Whenever you feel tempted to sacrifice too much, when the Con pops in to tell you you're not allowed to have what you want, you'll have your Harvest Strategy right there in front of you. It will remind you that you are getting exactly what you want out of your business.

The next time you're out to late-night dinner with Jack-of-All-Trades, remember the Most Valuable Positions you were looking at back at the office. You'll find it easy to ditch Jack and strategically focus your time by delegating everything else to your managers and their employees.

The Focused Business Map will remind you to cage or release your Gorillas and start focusing on hiring people with the traits your business needs to succeed. You will build a business of Most Valuable Employees.

When Ms. Opportunity pops in with a bag full of cubic zirconia to show off all the opportunities you're not exploiting, you'll be reminded of your Most Valuable Line. Instead of chasing "bright and shinies," you'll know that all the opportunity you need is right in front of you. Your Most Valuable Line will encourage you to redirect your entrepreneurial energies into things that are of most profit to your business.

When Siphon shows up, repelling her will be almost automatic. You'll know where to refer her, and, more important, how to cater more and more to the most profitable desires of your Most Valuable Customers.

Being reminded of your Most Valuable Message will stop the Jumbler dead in his tracks. You'll be able to use your marketing palette to paint a picture of your business that will lead a stampede of Most Valuable Customers through your front doors.

And you can ignore Overload when you're only looking at your five Most Valuable Indicators. No more analysis paralysis. Just strategic, focused action.

Your Next Chapter

As a focused entrepreneur, you have the power to do great things. You can create jobs. You can provide for your own. You can improve the quality of life for those around you. You can, in meaningful and tangible ways, make a difference in this world.

You can do all of this and more. You already had the gifts and skills necessary to make it happen. All you needed was a way to fend off the forces of chaos. Now nothing need stand in your way.

Be the hero. Be focused and take action.

I look forward to hearing about the next exciting chapter in your story . . .

BONUS MINI-BOOK!

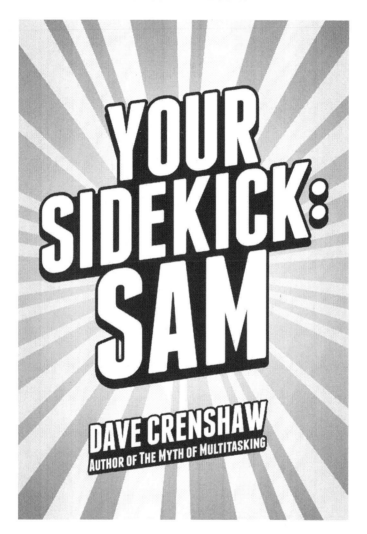

YOUR SIDEKICK, SAM

In *The Focused Business*, you learned the seven tools every heropreneur needs in his or her tool belt to triumph over Chaos.

There is an eighth tool, one that is so powerful that it deserves its own mini-book

I call it the SAM Cycle, which stands for Systems, Accountability, and Motivation. More about the acronym in a moment.

If you're the hero of this story, think of SAM as a trusty sidekick. He's there to do the bulk of the heavy lifting for you, so you can show up, flash a winning smile, and get all the glory. If you're a fan of *Lord of the Rings*, then just know that this SAM is that Sam to your Frodo.

The SAM Cycle has become the linchpin of my business coaching. It is the result of gradual refinement going back to when I first began coaching in 1998. It's so important that I actually *trademarked* the phrase, "Systems, Accountability, and Motivation." The SAM Cycle is so incredibly simple to understand, yet massively powerful in its implication for entrepreneurs.

Simply put, any issue in any small business can be quickly and accurately diagnosed using the SAM Cycle. It's that easy, and it's that powerful.

WHAT'S BUGGING YOU?

To prepare you to truly understand the power of the SAM cycle, I want you to pick a frustration.

What's the single biggest thing about your business that's just driving you nuts? That you wish you could change, improve, or just make disappear?

Most entrepreneurs have that problem on memory speed dial. But in case you need some help, here are some of the more common issues I've seen:

- *Employee discipline*
- *Poor sales*
- *Hiring issues*
- *Miscommunication*
- *Maintenance breakdowns*
- *Angry customers*
- *Production errors*
- *and so on . . .*

Right now, I'd like you to write that one frustration down. This is critical for you to get the most out of this chapter.

MY BUSINESS FRUSTRATION:

_____

_____

Got it? Mark this page, because we're going to come back to this frustration in a moment. But first, let's break down the components of the SAM Cycle.

SYSTEMS

S stands for Systems.

What the heck is a system? In short, systems are processes, tools, programs, hardware, scripts, apps, procedures . . . really anything you use in an effort to get a consistent result. Walk into most any large successful chain of stores and you'll see systems everywhere you look.

Starbucks? Systems.

Walmart? Systems.

Apple? Systems all over the place!

By my definition, Systems specifically have three important components: Results, Documents, and Tools.

- **RESULTS**
- **DOCUMENTS**
- **TOOLS**

RESULTS–First and foremost, we need to create a written definition of the result a system should create. For instance, if I'm documenting a system about greeting customers, then I might define the result as, "To make sure customers feel welcome and a part of the family." The result should *always* be more important than the process.

This means that defining the result is critical, because the result creates flexibility. Ever spoken to one of those answering services run in some distant hideout on the other side of the world? "Thank . . . you . . . sir . . . or . . . madam . . . for . . . calling . . . Happy . . . Store . . . where . . . we . . . are . . . happy . . . to . . . serve . . . you . . . May . . . I . . . first . . . have . . . your . . . fourteen . . . digit . . . account . . . number?" That is a perfect example of where the process was given more emphasis than the result. It's also a perfect example of everything that was wrong with business automation in the eighties and nineties.

No, now your customers expect more. They've had the experience of calling companies like Zappos and speaking to employees who, yes, are well-trained, but are also FLEXIBLE enough to give you real, human ATTENTION. They actually LISTEN to you instead of rattling off a script. Wow! Imagine that.

Remember: the result should always be defined first, because the result is always more important than the process.

DOCUMENTS–Documents are the recorded version of the system. It doesn't matter whether the format is paper or digital, written or video. It just needs to be a reference employees can use. Something that looks and seems tangible to them.

Now, over the years, I've noticed a very funny thing about business owners. Entrepreneurs tend to believe that systems are created the moment they think about them. This tendency is aggravating to your employees, who are often expected to, first, magically know what is going on in your mind and, second, remember the system you created, permanently, after only hearing it once.

Say the following out loud: "As if by magic, what I think becomes reality the second I think it."

See how silly it sounds when you read it? Then stop acting like it's true. Document your systems! Write everything down, starting with the results you expect your processes to create for your business. Implement the system more effectively by writing it down. It's that easy.

To recap, when is a system created?

Not the moment you dream it up. Nor the moment after. It is not created at the moment of conception. It is created as soon as you write it down, as soon as you put pen to paper with it. Nobody on earth can be held accountable to what is going on in your insane-entrepreneur brain, so you have to write it all down and show it to your employees before you can even think of holding them accountable to it.

Systems are created at the moment of documentation, not inception.

TOOLS–The term tool can be used to describe any implement that helps you or your employees complete a system. Remember, a system is a documented process with very clearly defined results. A tool is part of the process.

Think about it in terms of a highly simplified carpentry business. The artist's sketch is the result, a blueprint is the document, and the hammer is the tool. The hammer helps him build things. A carpenter uses the hammer, among many other tools, to follow the building system.

In your business, there are many tools at your disposal. Projectors. Documents. Books. Articles. Hardware. Software. Apps. This book is a tool for entrepreneurs. A tool can be something as general as an article you found in *Newsweek* that you would like your employees to read because it illustrates a certain point you find useful.

It is very important to make sure you get the right tool for the job. You do not want to have a hammer on hand if you're an ER surgeon . . . unless you want to give your patient a great excuse to sue you for malpractice!

Also, make sure you have the best quality tools possible. This will make it easier for your employees to get the results you want. Expecting them to complete spreadsheets on a six-year-old computer is like asking a 105-year-old Michael Jordan to slam-dunk the ball. The spirit is willing but the tool is weak.

So, identify the best tools. Get the best tools. Use the best tools.

ACCOUNTABILITY

A stands for Accountability.

Allow me to be crystal clear in my definition here. I define Accountability as a one-to-one relationship between you and someone else. Accountability requires a third party in order for it to be successful. So, while we can, individually, be personally *responsible* for our own actions, we can all benefit from making ourselves **ACCOUNTABLE** to another person.

Perhaps you've heard great athletes say that they're the product of great coaching? This illustrates the power of accountability. There's tremendous value in having someone who can assess what you're doing, give you training and support, and follow up on the progress that you're making.

The one-to-one aspect of accountability is essential. While there is a time and a place for group training and group meetings, these only serve to support systems.

In order to be as successful as you can possibly be as an entrepreneur, you want to cultivate one-to-one relationships in two directions:

- You holding a manager or employee individually accountable

- You making yourself accountable to a third party, usually a coach or mentor

Like Systems, Accountability has three major components: Trust, Training, and Follow-up.

- **TRUST**
- **TRAINING**
- **FOLLOW-UP**

TRUST – Trust is a question of relationship. If you're making yourself accountable to someone else, you must be sure you trust their guidance in your area of improvement. In other words, if you're trying to improve your golf swing, you're going to want to find a golf coach who has a reputation of being successful in helping golfers improve. If you're working with a business coach, you'll need to have confidence that coach is the kind of person who can help you and your business grow.

How about the flip side? If you're managing employees, do they trust you? Are they confident that you have their best interests at heart? This is usually where most managers and entrepreneurs unfortunately fall a bit short. They manage from the interest of the business, not the individual. This actually erodes trust over time.

If you want people to trust you, you're going to need to lead them and teach them from a standpoint of how it benefits THEM. If you want them to follow a system, why is it in their interest to follow that system? If you can consistently answer that question correctly, you'll go a long way toward building trust in others.

TRAINING – Once trust is established, now the coach or manager can provide ongoing training. In the simplest terms, training is any kind of instruction that helps a person improve. Your employees need ongoing and, occasionally, repetitive training.

Repetition and practice are powerful tools in helping people improve because they create conditioning. I first learned about conditioning in a very unlikely place—the banjo. Believe it or not, I was once a darn good banjo player. In high school, that was my nickname: Banjo. It's amazing I even got a prom date! Yet, in learning how to play the banjo, I had a good teacher who, through repetition and practice, helped me turn learned skills into automatic skills. This freed me up to be more creative in the moment, instead of worrying about where my fingers went. My fingers flew, and the ladies swooned at my five-string mastery.

Now, on a sidenote, I did eventually stop playing the banjo. Why? Well, to quote Steve Martin, there's one phrase that's never been uttered in the history of the world: "Oh, look, there's the banjo player's Porsche!" But I digress.

My point is, when it comes to training your employees—or being trained by someone else—embrace repetition. It's a powerful teacher.

FOLLOW-UP–If you are to successfully delegate tasks to other people, you must follow up. Follow-up is the most often neglected aspect of accountability when it comes to small business. As the owner, you delegate—but so often fail to follow up. The result is that employees forget that you care and eventually just stop doing what is expected.

Karl Pearson, English mathematician, has been credited with the following phrase:

That which is measured improves. That which is measured and reported improves exponentially.

When you make regular reporting and follow-up a part of accountability, your likelihood of success will improve dramatically. Always follow up.

Motivation

M is for Motivation.

What is motivation? In a small business context, it has little to do with Chris Farley living in a "van down by the river" or some high-energy speaker getting you pumped up.

Motivation is, simply, the reason people do what they do. It's the "why" behind their actions.

FACT: YOUR EMPLOYEES ALREADY ARE MOTIVATED.

If you're thinking about some of your employees, and you're thinking, "No way, Dave. No way these people are motivated. They didn't do squat today," then my reply is that they were motivated to do nothing today. The question isn't whether or not your employees are motivated. No, the real question is, what are they motivated to DO?

How well are you connecting their personal motivation to the results you want in your business? If those two things are not connected, if what your employees want most out of life cannot be hitched to your business needs, then—by golly—you will never get them motivated! Never!

The good news is, you absolutely can make that connection with the help of three components of Motivation: Vision, Values, and Cause.

- **VISION**
- **VALUES**
- **CAUSE**

VISION–Vision is a projection of what you want in the future. From a business perspective, you must have a documented vision of what you want in the future. Creating this written vision is a motivator not just for you, but for your employees as well. They want to see that they are a part of a company that is going somewhere—hopefully somewhere great!

For a personal perspective, each person also has a vision of what they want in the future. Ideally, this personal vision is written, as well. The clearer you make that vision to your employees, the easier it will be to help them stay motivated. You'll be able to connect daily action, or inaction, with personal long-term goals. For instance, "Alex, I notice that you've shown up late a few times in a row. I'm concerned because that's not behavior that fits with your vision of becoming a full-partner in the future."

When both you and your employees are clear about the vision, motivation comes naturally.

VALUES–Values are what you believe in the most. From a business perspective, values are the backbone of your culture. The greatest workplaces in the world almost always have a set of clearly defined, written values that form the basis of management and decision making every day.

From a personal perspective, values are what matter most to a person. Like a fingerprint or a snowflake, personal values are unique to each person. Pop quiz: do you know what matters most in the lives of every employee you manage? Do you know that by heart? Knowing the unique values of each person gives you a massive head start in becoming a motivational leader.

CAUSE–The last component, but certainly not the least, is having a cause. A cause is something greater than money. I've found that establishing a clear company cause unites your employees.

It gives them something greater than the needs and wants of the company, or even their own needs and wants.

Sometimes a company's cause can be directly related to your industry or target market, such as the Ronald McDonald houses for children, or Invaluable Inc.'s favorite causes, Kiva and Defy Ventures for entrepreneurs.[11] Other times the cause can be unrelated but something the company is passionate about, such as (Product) Red to fight AIDS, supported by Apple, Gap, and many others.

Regardless of the cause your business supports, if it is genuine and a part of the ongoing culture of your business, you will find a natural connection begins to grow between the hearts of your employees and the business they work for.

THE BUSINESS FRUSTRATION PROCESSING SYSTEM

Hopefully at this point we're on the same page regarding the SAM cycle. My guess is, as you read the previous sections, already a few lightbulbs flashed in your mind about actions you can take to fight chaos in your business. But we're just getting to the juicy part!

Remember that frustration you wrote down? Now we're going to find the solution.

On the next page you'll see a document I share with all of my clients, called the Business Frustration Processing System. This document by itself is worth the cost of this book . . . times 1,672,456 . . . rounded up.

---

11. See the back pages of this book to learn about our causes.

IDENTIFY ONE FRUSTRATION

HAS IT HAPPENED MORE THAN ONCE?

If NO, ignore it. If YES, proceed to the next step.

DEFINE THE RESULT YOU WANT

"Instead of X, I want Y."

GET TO THE ROOT OF THE PROBLEM USING THE SAM CYCLE

SYSTEMS

☐ Are there documented systems to deal with this?
☐ Are the systems accurate and up-to-date?
☐ Have responsibilities clearly been defined?
☐ Do people have the tools they need to succeed?

ACCOUNTABILITY

☐ Are results being measured?
☐ Is training being provided to teach correct actions?
☐ How consistent and effective is the follow-up?
☐ Are 1:1 meetings being held?
☐ Does the employee trust their manager?

MOTIVATION

☐ Does the employee want to work at your company?
☐ Have the company values been defined?
☐ Does the employee believe in the company values?
☐ Does the employee have a vision for their career?

WHAT IS THE NEXT ACTION?

Gather it . . .

PROCESS USING WHAT, WHEN, WHERE

Also, we've set up a web page where you can download a free copy of both this system and a blank worksheet for convenient printing. You're welcome. Go to **FOCUSEDBUSINESS.COM/FRUSTRATION**.

This system is so powerful that I require my clients to practice it with me, out loud, no less than twenty-one times over the course of our coaching. The point of all this repetition—there's that word again—is to make using this system a leadership habit.

How do you use it? Simple. Identify your frustration at step one, then work your way down through the system, answering each question.

HAS IT HAPPENED MORE THAN ONCE?

Don't skip this question, because it's critical. If the answer is, "yes!" then we can move to the next step.

However, if it's the first time it has happened, then let it go.[12] Ignore it. Your first reaction is to fix the problem, yet if it has only happened once, or occurs infrequently, then it's an incident—not a pattern. A good rule to follow:

IGNORE INCIDENTS.
PROCESS PATTERNS.

---

12. Unless, of course, it's something egregious, like someone selling drugs on the premises. But I've found this to be atypical to most business frustrations.

Why? Well, most people recognize when they screw up, and most people will correct their mistakes. And sometimes, weird things happen for no particular reason. If you spend loads of time and energy trying to solve a problem that's not really a problem, then you're wasting your time.

Define the Result You Want

The second step is to define the result you want. If, for example, your employees are regularly annoying you, and that's not the result you want, then you have to define the result you want.

You want them to stop being annoying. Say it out loud: "Instead of my employees being annoying, I want them to be pleasant to work with." Define the result.

If you are tired of getting lackluster sales, then state that result, as specifically as you can. "Instead of dropping leads, we want to have a 75 percent conversion rate."

The more specific you can be about the result, the easi ill be to eventually find the solution to your frustration.

Getting to The Root

Now it's time to ask questions. A lot of them. The more questions you ask, the better. Be relentless in asking yourself the questions related to the SAM Cycle. Even if you think you've discovered the answer in the System section of questions, KEEP GOING! You may uncover other, deeper root causes in Accountability and Motivation.

Keep in mind that the questions listed in this section are suggestions only. You may find that they don't exactly fit, have already been answered previously, or that the wording needs to be adjusted. Use them as a springboard to ask other, deeper questions.

Just make sure that you fully explore all aspects of the SAM Cycle before moving on to the next step.

WHAT IS THE NEXT ACTION?

After you go through the process of inquiry described in the Business Frustration Processing System, you will discover one action that your gut tells you will get the best results.

Just because you come up with six potential actions to help solve a problem doesn't mean you should try them all at the same time. That's part of what got you into this mess in the first place.

Remember the definition of focus? It's the strategic allocation of your resources toward that which is of most value.

So pick just the top idea of those six actions, or however many you came up with. Choose the one action most likely to get you the results you need.

As soon as you have it fixed in your mind, write down that action.[13]

PROCESS USING "WHAT, WHEN, WHERE"

You've decided what to do, but we're not quite done. Now you need to schedule time to take that action.

---

13.   If you're familiar with my Time Management training, then this is the time to put that action in an approved gathering point.

If you've read my book *Invaluable* or completed any of my Time Management courses, you'll know exactly what I mean when I say process using "What, When, Where." So do it!

For everyone else, the simplest explanation is, open up your calendar, determine how long it's going to take to complete that action, and schedule it. Then, when that time arrives, DO IT.

If you lack confidence in the area of using a calendar and following through on tasks, I recommend you visit **DAVECRENSHAW.COM/CHAOS**. Here you can take my free Chaos Assessment. Not only will this assessment give you an understanding of how much business and personal chaos you have, but it will also give you a custom-fit action plan to get the most appropriate help for your time management issues.

A FEW PARTING WORDS ABOUT SAM

If you're a part of a mastermind group—which is something I recommend—you can use this Frustration Processing System to discuss issues facing your business. Hearing each of these questions come from someone else will help you deal more objectively. This system will also help your group avoid "preaching to the choir." You know what I'm talking about, right? One hotshot entrepreneur thinks he knows all the answers and TELLS you what to do. Questions are much more persuasive and enlightening than instructions.

And that leads me to my final point.

Not only is the SAM Cycle important for **YOU** to know, it's vital that you teach it to your employees, too. At some point, very soon, call your group together and spend twenty minutes teaching them the SAM Cycle, exactly like I did here. It will be time well invested.

That way when they have a problem, instead of spending half the day trying to solve it for them, you can respond with, "Have you run it through the SAM Cycle, yet? Do that first, then come back to me with your thoughts."

As they go through the process, they will solve the vast majority of their problems on their own. This will save you a lot of time.

Now that you've got your trusty sidekick, let's go do battle with the forces of Chaos!

GLOSSARY

ACCOUNTABILITY – a one-to-one relationship—such as between an employee and manager or entrepreneur and coach—that ensures systems are being followed and a person's individual motivation is being satisfied; in the SAM or Invaluable Cycle, Accountability is composed of mutual trust, ongoing training, and consistent follow-up

AGENT OF CHAOS – a fictitious personification of an aspect of Chaos that is common to entrepreneurs; see the Con, Jack-of-All-Trades, the Gorilla, Ms. Opportunity, Siphon, the Jumbler, and Overload

CAUSE – a higher, nobler purpose that an individual or company supports beyond just making a profit

CHAOS – the haphazard allocation of your resources toward that which is of variable value

CHAOS INC. – the fictitious organization whose primary purpose is to destroy small businesses and frustrate entrepreneurs; acronym for Company Havoc And Owner Stress

CON, THE – the fictitious Agent of Chaos who convinces entrepreneurs to sacrifice money, time, and relationships for an elusive Ultimate Harvest that is ever in the future

DOCUMENTS – a physical or digital record of how a system should be completed; documents can include printed operation manuals, company wikis, video, audio recording, and so on; until a system is documented, it does not exist

FOCUS – the strategic allocation of your resources toward that which is of most value

FOCUSED BUSINESS MAP – the single-page tool that an entrepreneur can use daily, showing the progress of their targets in the

Seven Focus Tools and also their progress in growing their business

FOCUSED BUSINESS MODEL – a pattern and philosophy followed by the world's most successful entrepreneurs; focus leads to mastery leads to diversification

FOLLOW-UP – the consistent requirement of a manager or coach to check in with someone they serve and make sure that they're completing assigned tasks; includes reporting, delegation, and tracking over time

FRUSTRATION – a pattern of events that causes negative results in a business

FRUSTRATION PROCESSING – a systematic approach to handling frustrations with a business; involves analyzing a business frustration in terms of Systems, Accountability, and Motivation (the SAM Cycle)

GORILLA, THE – the fictitious Agent of Chaos who represents strong employees who bring great value but create messes throughout the business; typically, Gorillas are family, friends, or employees who have been with a business for a long period of time

HARVEST STRATEGY – an entrepreneur's written definition of the benefits that they want to receive from their business on a daily, weekly, monthly, yearly, and ultimate basis; includes definition of both personal and family benefits

JACK-OF-ALL-TRADES – a fictitious Agent of Chaos whose purpose is to cause entrepreneurs to continually multitask and never delegate responsibilities to employees

JUMBLER, THE – a fictitious Agent of Chaos who causes mental confusion, usually for the entrepreneur, as how to best communicate with potential customers

LINE – short for product or service line; a category of products or services that you sell

MS. OPPORTUNITY – the fictitious Agent of Chaos who distracts you with opportunities, projects, and premature diversification

MOTIVATION – the purpose that drives an individual; motivation cannot be given to another person, but instead can be identified within that person and connected to their day-to-day actions; in the SAM Cycle, motivation is composed of a person's long-term vision, their deeply held values, and a cause that they believe in

MVB (MOST VALUABLE BUSINESS) – if an entrepreneur has multiple businesses in play at the moment, the Most Valuable Business is the one that brings the greatest profit and personal satisfaction; an entrepreneur should focus on their MVB and find a way to disengage or delegate responsibilities for all other businesses

MVC (MOST VALUABLE CUSTOMER) – the customer who is most likely to buy your Most Valuable Line of products and services (MVL); target market

MVE (MOST VALUABLE EMPLOYEE) – a person who possesses a combination of traits that makes them most likely to succeed in your business regardless of position

MVI (MOST VALUABLE INDICATORS) – the five numbers most critical to your small business success; includes cash on hand, profit, your salary, and two more of your choosing

MVL (MOST VALUABLE LINE) – the category of product or service that your business sells that is most valuable in terms of profit, alignment with values, and personal enjoyment

MVP (MOST VALUABLE POSITION) – the one position within the organization chart that an entrepreneur should focus on; when the entrepreneur works in this position, they provide maximum value to the business

OVERLOAD – the fictitious Agent of Chaos who bombards you with so much information you don't know what to do or who to listen to; her main tool is analysis paralysis; short for information overload

RESULT – the clear definition of what the outcome of a system should be; the result is the "why" and "what" of a system and matters more than the individual steps

SAM CYCLE (OR INVALUABLE CYCLE) – the master system for all businesses; the repeated cycle and relationship between Systems, Accountability, and Motivation; any problem within the business can be traced back to either a lack of or improper implementation of one of these three things

SEVEN FOCUS TOOLS – the seven specific tools that an entrepreneur can use and review on a daily basis to make sure that they stay focused and keep chaos at bay; see Harvest Strategy, MVP, MVE, MVL, MVC, MVM, and MVI

SIPHON – the fictitious Agent of Chaos representing customers who ask for exceptions and require much more from the business than they give in return

SKILL – knowledge, experience, or expertise of an employee; can be taught with some time and investment after hiring an employee; the "would like" portion of the hiring process

SYSTEMS – a documented process or procedure intended to get consistent results within a business; in the SAM Cycle, systems are composed of defined results, physical documents, and helpful tools

TASK PROCESSING – the act of taking one item from a gathering point and deciding what the next step is, when it will be done, and where its home is; covered in depth in Dave Crenshaw's time management training; What, When, Where Processing

TOOL – a supporting document, physical implement, or piece of software that helps someone complete a system yet does not necessarily show how something should be done; a hammer or an article about good communication skills are both tools

TRAINING – the ongoing scheduled improvement provided in an accountability relationship

TRAIT – a personality characteristic of an employee, something that you cannot teach or would be very difficult to teach; considered "must have" in the hiring process

TRUST – the respect you give someone else in an accountability relationship and the confidence you have in them to help you achieve the results that you want in business and in life

VALUES – the principles an individual or business uses to guide how they act and operate on a daily basis

VISION – an individual's or company's defined, big end result; see Harvest Strategy

SPECIAL THANKS

I remember the good old days when sitcoms often started with the announcement: "This show was filmed in front of a live studio audience." Well, this book was, in a sense, written in front of a live audience, too.

At a private retreat of small business owners, I laid out, for the first time, the contents of *The Focused Business*. The attendees were all at various stages of business development and came from a variety of industries. However, they all had an impact on the development of this book. I sincerely thank each of these business owners and would encourage you to frequent their businesses. Tell them Dave sent you.

Ann Colin
DanceWorks
danceworks.us

Jennifer Duffield
Dancing Moose Montessori School
mydancingmoose.com

Angy Ford
Bravo Arts Academy
utahbravo.com

Darin Harker
Quirk
Quirkinc.com

Jason Hewlett
Jason Hewlett Entertainment
jasonhewlett.com

Jacob Hoehne
Issimo Productions
IssimoProductions.com

Jim Holbrook
Premier Plastics Inc.
premierplastics.net

David Hunter and Chris Dexter
Dexter & Dexter,
Attorneys at Law
DexterLaw.com

Rebecca Lowe
Centerstage Academy
SpotlightonCenterstage.com

Jacquelyn Ormsbee
Best Connections
weconnectbest.com

Yong Pratt
Academy of the Arts
ElkoArtsAcademy.com

Angie and Ryan Snow
Western Heating & Air
Conditioning
WesternHeatingAir.com

Liliana Somma
School of Dance & Music
SchoolOfDanceAndMusic.com

Stacy Tuschl
The Academy of
Performing Arts
academywi.com

Shannon Wilson
Westwoods Center of
Performing Arts
centerofperformingarts.org

ALSO DESERVING OF MANY THANKS

Aston Reynolds — my awesome editor/writing assistant extraordinaire

John, Faye, and Aimee — you are truly invaluable and make my job so much easier

Olivia Merrill — for the attention to the fine editing details I always miss

Winford — the evolution has come full circle

Matt Wagner — for believing in my first book and for having unwavering integrity

Katherine — for putting up with my entrepreneurial insanity

All of my clients, past, present, and future — for allowing me to serve you and, in the process, learn both with and from you

INVALUABLE INC.'s CAUSE

Contrary to popular belief, and largely thanks to my wife and kids, I no longer have delusions of world domination. My cause is a lot simpler than that these days.

My overarching cause, the one that drives my business, is simply to *save entrepreneurs from chaos*. I believe that helping new entrepreneurs succeed is not a handout, but a hand up. Entrepreneurship empowers people to solve their own problems, rise from poverty, and create opportunity for those around them.

There are two ventures I admire because I think they make a big difference in the world of entrepreneurship.

The first is **KIVA**. Kiva allows you to make small loans to other entrepreneurs around the world. It's so easy and so simple to make a micro-loan and, since it will be repaid, your investment can then be passed on to the next micro-entrepreneur. Go here to get started: **DAVECRENSHAW.COM/KIVA**

I am also very passionate about an organization called **DEFY VENTURES** that teaches entrepreneurship to convicts. A lot of people who go to prison come out with literally zero opportunity. Comfortable employing a convicted felon? That's what I thought. The only chance a lot of these guys have when they get out is either get back into crime or start a legitimate business. Defy teaches them the skills they'll need to create their own opportunities, which is what entrepreneurship is all about. For a lot of those guys, it's exactly the second chance they need— one they can take full responsibility for, without looking to outside sources for a handout. Learn more and donate to Defy at: **DAVECRENSHAW.COM/DEFY**

Please join with me in supporting these worthy causes.

FREE CHAOS ASSESSMENT

GET RESULTS NOW!

Continue your journey and find out what your personal brand of professional chaos looks like. Take Dave Crenshaw's free Chaos Assessment and receive your personalized action plan.

Think of the assessment as a mirror; the action plan you will receive is the reflection. Your answers are always confidential, and every personalized action plan is just that—handcrafted by a specialist to help you triumph over chaos.

Take action now by completing your confidential chaos assessment at:

CHAOSQUIZ.COM

Your free action plan will land in your inbox within one business day, full of specific, hard-hitting advice that will help you make a difference at your business.

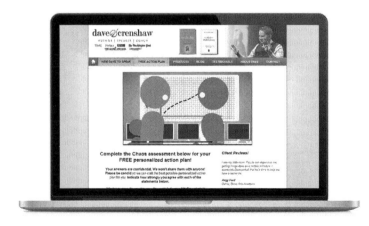